DEF COUNTY F.C.

- THE 25 YEAR RECORD

1970-71 to 1994-95 Seasons

SEASON BY SEASON WRITE-UPS
David Powter

EDITOR
Michael Robinson

CONTENTS

British Library Cataloguing in Publication Data
A catalogue record for this book is available from the British Library
ISBN 0-947808-57-4

Printed by Redwood Books, Kennet House, Kennet Way, Trowbridge, Wilts.

DERBY COUNTY
- Seasons 1970-71 to 1994-95

After their fourth successive failure to secure promotion back to the top-flight, Derby County appointed a new manager, Jim Smith, at the end of 1994-95. Twenty five seasons earlier, in 1970-71, the club had just completed their first term in the top-flight since 1953. That first season back under Brian Clough (and his assistant Peter Taylor) had been a very successful one as they had finished a creditable 4th; and much was expected from the next campaign.

1970-71 kicked off well as they won the pre-season Watney Cup tournament (beating Manchester United in the final). Their League prospects remained bright following a good start, but 7 defeats in September and October knocked them backwards. However, the Rams gradually regained form and finished 9th.

The influential skipper Dave Mackay moved to Swindon in the summer of 1971, but Derby hardly missed him, making a marvellous start with a 12 game unbeaten run. They were never far from the top-spot and seven victories in March and April gave County a golden opportunity of taking the title. However, defeats at home to Newcastle and at Manchester City reduced their chances before a crucial 1-0 victory over Liverpool sent them to the top of the table on completion of their 42 games. Both Leeds (needing one point) and Liverpool (needing a win) could overtake Derby to win the Championship, and each had one more fixture to complete. However, Leeds were defeated and Liverpool could only draw, so Derby County were handed their first League title.

The nucleus of that first Championship winning squad was Colin Boulton (the goalkeeper), Ron Webster, John Robson, Roy McFarland, Colin Todd, Terry Hennessey, Archie Gemmill, John McGovern, Alan Durban, Alan Hinton (the top scorer with 15 goals), John O'Hare and Kevin Hector. County also won the Texaco Cup in 1971-72, beating Airdrieonians over two legs in the final.

Derby made a poor defence of their title, winning only one of their first 6 games. Their form hardly improved until December when they gradually worked their way into the top ten. Their 1972-73 finish was 7th, Hector top scoring with 14.

The club had its best FA Cup run since 1950, before losing 1-0 to Leeds at the Baseball Ground in the quarter-final. They went one round further in their first European Cup campaign, side-stepping Zeljeznicar Sarajevo, Benfica and Spartak Trnava; but eventually losing gallantly - and controversially - to Juventus.

1973-74 started promisingly and County were in third place after winning at Old Trafford on 13th October; however, 2 days later, the football world was rocked by the resignations of Clough and Taylor. This followed a disagreement between Clough and his chairman Sam Longson. The latter resisted all attempts to get the management duo reinstated, saying "We will go into the Second Division with our heads in the air rather than winning the First Division wondering whether the club will be expelled from the Football League." The players also expressed their view and wanted Clough and Taylor to return. They even staged a sit-in after it was announced that Dave Mackay was to be the new manager. However, after initially threatening not to play at West Ham, the players relented and the game ended 0-0.

After a brief dip in form, the Rams improved to finish third, 14 points behind the Champions Leeds. Mackay's first two signings were Rod Thomas (from Swindon) and Bruce Rioch (from Villa).

Despite signing Manchester City forward Francis Lee in the close season, there was little expectation of a title success in 1974-75. A mediocre start appeared to underline this and they were only 14th in mid-September.

While their League form slowly improved, a UEFA Cup run gained momentum with victories over Servette and Atletico Madrid. However, Velez surprised them in the third round by taking the lead in the first leg at the Baseball Ground. Derby fought back to win 3-1 on the night, but lost the return 4-1 in Yugoslavia and exited on aggregate.

With no further foreign travel to distract them, Mackay's side concentrated on boosting their League position. They were only on the fringe of the title race in mid-March, but produced a great run to cut through the fancied clubs to go top of the table for the first time on 12th April. Seven days later Derby had virtually won the title after drawing at Leicester, as all their rivals (Liverpool, Ipswich and Everton) were defeated. The title was actually clinched when Ipswich dropped a point, at Maine Road, in their next game. The Rams finished 2 points ahead of Liverpool (and Ipswich) with 53 points - the lowest Champions' total in 20 years.

Rioch was the top scorer with 15, while Hector netted 13 and Lee and Roger Davies (including 5 in one game) contributed 11 apiece. The fulcrum of the side was the outstanding midfield trio of Rioch, Gemmill and Henry

Old Derby players view the Championship Trophy
displayed at the Baseball Ground in 1975.

Newton. David Nish, a Clough signing like Newton, and Peter Daniel were both solid in defence along with Webster and Todd. Daniel deputised for McFarland, whose season was restricted to just the final 4 games because of injury.

Dave Mackay strengthened his squad by signing Charlie George before the start of the new season. However, Derby suffered a shock start to the defence of their title with an embarrassing 5-1 defeat by QPR in their opening home game. Five wins in 6 games put the Rams back on course and a similar spell in November sent them to the top of the table. However, Mackay's side were not able to maintain their challenge and had to be content with 4th, 7 points behind the Champions Liverpool.

Undoubtedly a contributory factor to the loss of their crown was the distraction of a lengthy FA Cup run. County triumphed 4 times at home to set up a Hillsborough meeting with Manchester United. However, the club's first semi-final for 30 years ended disappointingly with a 2-0 defeat.

Earlier in 1975-76, their European Cup run was halted dramatically in the second round. There were high expectations when George netted a hat-trick in the 4-1 victory against Real Madrid in the first leg. However, it was a different story at the Bernabeu, with an identical score-line in the Spaniards' favour after 90 minutes. Mackay's braves were then defeated by a 5th goal in extra-time.

The club made an awful start to 1976-77, picking up only 5 points from the first eight fixtures. Remarkably, the Rams then turned on the style and thrashed Spurs 8-2 at the Baseball Ground, Rioch netting 4 times. However, just over a month later, Dave Mackay (and his assistant Des Anderson) resigned after the board refused to give him a vote of confidence. Reserve team coach Colin Murphy stepped up to take the reins, initially as caretaker but, after some promising results, on a permanent basis.

Although the club sank to the bottom of the table in early March, a fine spell containing just 2 defeats from the final 15 matches enabled them to climb to 15th. Gerry Daly's arrival from Manchester United had made a positive impact; but Murphy's other big buy - striker Derek Hales - was struggling to settle in.

In contrast to their early League form in 1976-77, Derby had embarked on another good FA Cup run; it came to a halt in the quarter-final when Everton defeated them 2-0 at Goodison Park.

County got off to another bad start in 1977-78 and, after gathering just 2 points from 5 games, Murphy was relieved of his managerial role and replaced by Tommy Docherty. Murphy (and his coach Dario Gradi) left the Baseball Ground soon afterwards, as did Gemmill (who joined Clough at Forest) and Hales who was despatched to West Ham for a cut-price fee.

Docherty completely shook the side up, bringing in John Middleton (as keeper, in part-exchange for Gemmill), Don Masson (from QPR), Steve Buckley (from Luton), Terry Curran (from Forest) and, at the end of the season, Gordon Hill (from Manchester United). By the time Hill made his scoring debut in the 3-0 home win over Arsenal on the season's final day, Docherty's rejigged side were secure in 12th.

Docherty's first and only full season as manager of Derby was far from successful. The fans were unhappy that the old title winning side had been dismantled too quickly, especially as the replacements generally appeared inadequate. Hill started 12 games and Rioch only 8, while Todd and George were early season departures.

The struggle persisted all through the campaign and they just survived relegation, in 19th, by one place and 6 points. A lack of goals was undoubtedly a major problem, Daly top scoring with 13 out of only 44. Tommy Docherty resigned shortly after the end of 1978-79 and was replaced by Colin Addison.

Addison's side got off to a mediocre start, which was compounded by a bad injury to McFarland in a 4-0 defeat at Southampton. In a bid to improve matters Addison recruited Steve Emery (from Hereford), Roger Davies (for his second spell on his return from the USA) and the Coventry pair of Keith

Osgood and Barry Powell. But things just went from bad to worse in the 1979-80 season as only one point was gained from a 9 game spell either side of Christmas. Derby remained in the relegation zone until the end of the season, finishing 21st, 5 points from safety. The new year signing of strikers Alan Biley and David Swindlehurst had come too late to save them. Biley top scored with 9 (out of a total of 47) from 18 games.

Derby made a good start to 1980-81 with 4 wins from the first 6 Second Division fixtures. However, a glut of draws slowed them down and, despite never falling out of the top half, they were unable to stay in contention for promotion - finishing 6th, 5 points out of the frame.

The axe fell on Colin Addison's reign at the Baseball Ground the following January. His side had struggled from the start in 1981-82 and were lying in 13th on his departure. His assistant, John Newman, took over and they finished 16th. Kevin Hector made his last appearance for the club in the final

The Derby County team photo from the 1982/83 Season

day victory over Watford. The goal he netted in that game brought his total to 155 from a club record number of 486 League games (over 2 spells).

There was no improvement at the start of the following term; only one of the first 13 games was won and Newman, too, was dismissed. Peter Taylor was persuaded out of retirement to form a management team with Roy McFarland and Mick Jones. The latter pair were enticed from Bradford City, where McFarland had managed successfully since leaving the Baseball Ground.

Gradually Derby's form improved and, with Gemmill returning to bolster the midfield, a fine 15 game unbeaten run took them to safety and a 1982-83 finish of 13th.

The only highlight of 1983-84 was an FA Cup run which ultimately ended in disappointment. Cambridge United, Telford United and First Division Norwich were all beaten; but then, with a semi-final beckoning, Derby crashed to a goal direct from a corner-kick by Third Division Plymouth in a Baseball Ground replay.

If that FA Cup exit was a major disappointment, County's League campaign was an absolute disaster. The Rams only scored more than once on 7 occasions, netting just 36 in total. Peter Taylor lured John Robertson from Nottingham Forest, but neither he, Gemmill nor former England defender Dave Watson could make up for the squad's many deficiencies.

Having dropped into the bottom three in mid January, County found it impossible to dig themselves out of trouble, especially as there were many distractions off the pitch. The club was in serious financial trouble and Robert Maxwell stepped in to help pay off a tax debt by buying the Baseball Ground.

The first act of the new board was to axe Peter Taylor. Roy McFarland took over on a caretaker basis, but could not stave off relegation. The Rams finished 20th, 5 points from safety, with Bobby Davison top scoring with 14.

Arthur Cox was appointed manager during the close season with Roy

Derby County's Team from the 1984 Centenary Year

Back Row (left to right) : - Roy MacFarland (Assistant Manager)   Billy Livingstone
Paul Blades   Charlie Palmer   Rob Hindmarch   Eric Steele   Richard Pratley
Andy Garner   Mark Clifford   Steve Buckley   Gordon Guthrie (Physiotherapist)

Front Row (left to right) : - Steve Devine   Paul Hooks   Kevin Taylor
Bobby Davison   Kenny Burns   Arthur Cox (Manager)   Steve Powell
Kevin Wilson   John Robertson   Graham Harbey   Andy Irvine

McFarland reverting to assistant-manager. After a mediocre start, Cox's side struggled to make any impact on the promotion pace-setters and had to settle for a 1984-85 finish of 7th in Division Three.

Derby struggled to find any consistency in the early stages of 1985-86, but 5 successive victories lifted them into the chasing pack. They started 1986 in second place, but a wobble in March knocked them down to 5th, a position they held at the end of the last Saturday of the season. However, they then won 2 (out of 3) rearranged games to return to the second-flight after a gap of two seasons. Derby had finished third, 10 points behind the Champions Reading, and one point above Wigan, the unlucky 4th club.

Davison was the top scorer (with 19 goals) for the 4th consecutive time in the 1986-87 season, as Derby made it two promotions in two seasons. Five victories on the trot compensated for a mixed start and shortly after Christmas they were disputing top spot with Portsmouth. The two clubs slogged it out for the title, and it was the Rams who got their noses in front when it

**Bobby Davison in action for the Rams against Ipswich Town
during the 1986/87 Season**

mattered by winning 4 of their last 5 games. The gap between the two sides
was 6 points with Derby totalling 84 - a club record.

Even though the squad was strengthened by the arrival of the Southampton
pair Peter Shilton and Mark Wright, County found it heavy going in their
first term back in the top-flight. In particular, goals were at a premium,
although an unbeaten 5 game run pushed them into the top half of the table
in early December. However, this was followed by a disastrous spell of 8
successive defeats which sent them spiralling into the relegation zone. They
pulled out of their nose-dive just in time and an unbeaten run of 7 games
took them clear of trouble. County finished 15th in 1987-88, just one point
above the relegation play-off position.

1988-89 turned out to be the club's best for 13 seasons. However, few would
have expected it after they netted only 4 times in the first 8 games. Goals and

better results followed after close season recruits Paul Goddard and Trevor Hebberd had been joined by Ted McMinn and Dean Saunders. This Derby side was hardly flamboyant - they only scored 40 goals - but was very efficient, edging several games by the odd goal. They were in the top half of the table from November onwards and finished 5th.

Any hopes of a follow-up in 1989-90 were dashed by a bad start, and after 12 games they had only 3 teams below them. However, 4 straight wins lifted lifted them into the top six, but they could not maintain their form and slipped backwards. Several poor displays near the end of the season, when they won only 2 of their final 12 games, pushed them within 3 points of the relegation zone in 16th.

Derby were in trouble from the start of 1990-91 and did not win a League game until 27th October. That 1-0 success at the Dell was the start of their only good spell, which yielded 4 wins from 6 games. Immediately after-wards they lost 6-4 at home to Chelsea and then won only once more all season. That was the return game with Southampton (which ended 6-2); but by then it was too late. Derby were relegated in 20th and bottom place. They accumulated only 24 points and conceded 75 goals including 36 at the Baseball Ground (13 of which came in 2 games - including a 7-1 debacle at the hands of Liverpool). For the third term running, Saunders was the top scorer (with 17 out of a total of just 37).

A mixed start ensured that Derby were always chasing the leading pack in 1991-92; but a late burst of 6 wins from their last 7 fixtures lifted them to third and the promotion play-offs. Prospects of a trip to Wembley looked promising as the Rams took a 2 goal lead at Blackburn in the semi-final first leg, but their opponents fought back to take a 4-2 advantage to the Baseball Ground. County won that return 2-1 but Rovers progressed (ultimately to much better things) with an aggregate victory.

Another dreadful start ruined Derby's chances of promotion in 1992-93. They had to wait until the 8th game for their first win and were yet again chasing the pacemakers. Eight wins in eleven boosted their hopes, but a lack of consistency afterwards meant that Cox's expensively-assembled side got no higher than their finishing position of 8th, 10 points short of the play-offs. Their chances had been severely hampered by 10 defeats at the Baseball Ground.

Derby visited Wembley for the first time in 47 years in 1992-93, when they reached the final of the Anglo-Italian Cup. However, Serie B side Cremonese proved too good for them; Marco Gabbiadini netted the Rams' goal in the 3-1 defeat.

After 9 years at the club, Arthur Cox resigned through ill health in early 1993-94 and Roy McFarland stepped up to take the reins again. Although never among the automatic promotion places, County plugged away on the heels of the leaders. Their home form had improved, but they were now struggling on their travels. Nevertheless, McFarland's side finished 6th - qualifying for the play-offs by 3 points. Paul Kitson, Tommy Johnson and Gabbiadini were the joint top scorers with 13 each.

Derby qualified for a play-off final against Leicester by beating Millwall 2-0 at home and 3-1 at the Den. The second leg in London was interrupted by several pitch invasions and crowd disturbances. In the Wembley final, Johnson opened the scoring; but Leicester equalised and then broke Derby's hearts with a winner 3 minutes from time.

The disappointment continued into 1994-95 when County rarely looked like joining the promotion race. After his side finished the season in 9th, Roy McFarland was dismissed and shortly afterwards was replaced by Jim Smith.

The Baseball Ground pictured at the beginning of the 1995-96 Season.

F.A. CUP COMPETITION

1970/71 SEASON
3rd Round
Jan 2 vs Chester (a) 2-1
Att: 15,882 Wignall, Gemmill

4th Round
Jan 23 vs Wolverhampton Wands. (h) 2-1
Att: 40,567 Hinton (pen), O'Hare

5th Round
Feb 13 vs Everton (a) 0-1
Att: 53,490

1971/72 SEASON
3rd Round
Jan 15 vs Shrewsbury Town (h) 2-0
Att: 33,463 Hector 2

4th Round
Feb 5 vs Notts County (h) 6-0
Att: 39,450 Durban 3, Robson, Hector, Hinton (pen)

5th Round
Feb 26 vs Arsenal (h) 2-2
Att: 39,622 Durban, Hinton (pen)

Replay
Feb 29 vs Arsenal (a) 0-0 (aet.)
Att: 63,077

2nd Replay (at Filbert Street)
Mar 13 vs Arsenal 0-1
Att: 40,000

1972/73 SEASON
3rd Round
Jan 13 vs Peterborough United (a) 1-0
Att: 20,855 Davies

4th Round
Feb 3 vs Tottenham Hotspur (h) 1-1
Att: 37,895 Davies

Replay
Feb 7 vs Tottenham Hotspur (a) 5-3
Att: 52,736 Davies 3, Hector 2

5th Round
Feb 24 vs Queen's Park Rangers (h) 4-2
Att: 38,100 Hector 3, Davies

6th Round
Mar 17 vs Leeds United (h) 0-1
Att: 38,350

1973/74 SEASON
3rd Round
Jan 5 vs Boston United (h) 0-0
Att: 25,788

Replay
Jan 9 vs Boston United (a) 6-1
Att: 9,000 Gemmill 3 (1 pen), Bourne, Nish

4th Round
Jan 27 vs Coventry City (a) 0-0
Att: 40,885

Replay
Jan 30 vs Coventry City (h) 0-1 (aet.)
Att: 31,907

1974/75 SEASON
3rd Round
Jan 4 vs Orient (a) 2-2
Att: 12,490 Todd 2

Replay
Jan 8 vs Orient (h) 2-1
Att: 26,501 Lee, Rioch

4th Round
Jan 27 vs Bristol Rovers (h) 2-0
Att: 27,980 Hector, Rioch (pen)

5th Round
Feb 18 vs Leeds United (h) 0-1
Att: 35,298

1975/76 SEASON
3rd Round
Jan 3 vs Everton (h) 2-1
Att: 31,647 George 2

4th Round
Jan 24 vs Liverpool (h) 1-0
Att: 38,200 Davies

5th Round
Feb 14 vs Southend United (h) 1-0
Att: 31,918 Rioch

6th Round
Mar 6 vs Newcastle United (h) 4-2
Att: 38,362 Rioch 2, Newton, George

Semi-Final (at Hillsborough)
Apr 3 vs Manchester United 0-2
Att: 55,000

1976/77 SEASON
3rd Round
Jan 8 vs Blackpool (a) 0-0
Att: 19,442

Replay
Jan 19 vs Blackpool (h) 3-2
Att: 21,433 Hales, James, George

4th Round
Jan 29 vs Colchester United (a) 1-1
Att: 14,030 Hales

Replay
Feb 2 vs Colchester United (h) 1-0
Att: 22,155 James

5th Round
Feb 26 vs Blackburn Rovers (h) 3-1
Att: 30,439 George 2 (1 pen), Hector

6th Round
Mar 19 vs Everton (a) 0-2
Att: 42,409

1977/78 SEASON
3rd Round
Jan 7 vs Southend United (h) 3-2
Att: 23,625 Masson, Ryan, Young (og)

4th Round
Feb 1 vs Birmingham City (h) 2-1
Att: 31,955 Daly, Masson

5th Round
Feb 22 vs West Bromwich Albion (h) 2-3
Att: 32,698 Rioch 2

1978/79 SEASON
3rd Round
Jan 6 vs Preston North End (a) 0-3
Att: 19,884

1979/80 SEASON
3rd Round
Jan 5 vs Bristol City (a) 2-6
Att: 13,384 Davies, Daly

1980/81 SEASON
3rd Round
Jan 3 vs Bristol City (h) 0-0
Att: 19,071

Replay
Jan 7 vs Bristol City (a) 0-2
Att: 13,649

1981/82 SEASON
3rd Round
Jan 2 vs Bolton Wanderers (a) 1-3
Att: 9,534 Powell B

1982/83 SEASON
3rd Round
Jan 8 vs Nottingham Forest (h) 2-0
Att: 28,494 Gemmill, Hill

4th Round
Jan 29 vs Chelsea (h) 2-1
Att: 23,383 Wilson 2

5th Round
Feb 19 vs Manchester United (h) 0-1
Att: 33,022

1983/84 SEASON
3rd Round
Jan 7 vs Cambridge United (a) 3-0
Att: 6,309 Wilson, Plummer, McAlle

4th Round
Feb 1 vs Telford United (h) 3-2
Att: 21,488 Davison 3

5th Round
Feb 18 vs Norwich City (h) 2-1
Att: 25,793 Gemmill (pen), Davison

6th Round
Mar 10 vs Plymouth Argyle (a) 0-0
Att: 34,365

Replay
Mar 14 vs Plymouth Argyle (h) 0-1
Att: 26,906

1984/85 SEASON
1st Round
Nov 17 vs Hartlepool United (a) 1-2
Att: 7,431 Powell (pen)

1985/86 SEASON
1st Round
Nov 16 vs Crewe Alexandra (h) 5-1
Att: 11,047 Chandler (pen), Davison 2, Christie 2

2nd Round
Dec 9 vs Telford United (h) 6-1
Att: 12,267 Gregory, Chandler 3, Micklewhite 2

3rd Round
Jan 4 vs Gillingham (h) 1-1
Att: 8,983 Garner

Replay
Jan 13 vs Gillingham (h) 3-1
Att: 10,959 Micklewhite, Garner, Christie

4th Round
Jan 25 vs Sheffield United (a) 1-0
Att: 22,658 Hindmarch

5th Round
Feb 26 vs Sheffield Wednesday (h) 1-1
Att: 22,781 Davison

Replay
Mar 5 vs Sheffield Wednesday (a) 0-2
Att: 29,077

1986/87 SEASON
3rd Round
Jan 26 vs Sheffield Wednesday (a) 0-1
Att: 25,695

1987/88 SEASON
3rd Round
Jan 9 vs Chelsea (h) 1-3
Att: 18,753 Penney

1988/89 SEASON
3rd Round
Jan 7 vs Southampton (h) 1-1
Att: 17,178 Hebberd

Replay
Jan 10 vs Southampton (a) 2-1 (aet.)
Att: 16,323 McMinn, Callaghan

4th Round
Jan 28 vs Watford (a) 1-2
Att: 20,078 Micklewhite

1989/90 SEASON
3rd Round
Jan 7 vs Port Vale (a) 1-1
Att: 17,478 Hebberd

Replay
Jan 10 vs Port Vale (h) 2-3
Att: 21,389 Ramage, Francis

15

1990/91 SEASON
3rd Round
Jan 5 vs Newcastle United (a) 0-2
Att: 19,748

1991/92 SEASON
3rd Round
Jan 4 vs Burnley (a) 2-2
Att: 18,772 Chalk, Comyn
Replay
Jan 14 vs Burnley (h) 2-0
Game abandoned after 76 minutes due to fog
Replay
Jan 25 vs Burnley (h) 2-0
Att: 18,374 Williams P, Ormondroyd
4th Round
Feb 5 vs Aston Villa (h) 3-4
Att: 22,452 Gee 2, Williams P

1992/93 SEASON
3rd Round
Jan 2 vs Stockport County (h) 2-1
Att: 17,960 Short, Miller (og)
4th Round
Jan 23 vs Luton Town (a) 5-1
Att: 9,170 Short, Pembridge 3, Gabbiadini
5th Round
Feb 13 vs Bolton Wanderers (h) 3-1
Att: 20,289 Short 2, Williams
6th Round
Mar 8 vs Sheffield Wednesday (h) 3-3
Att: 22,511 Nicholson, Gabbiadini, Kitson
Replay
Mar 17 vs Sheffield Wednesday (a) 0-1
Att: 32,033

1993/94 SEASON
3rd Round
Jan 8 vs Oldham Athletic (a) 1-2
Att: 12,810 Johnson

1994/95 SEASON
3rd Round
Jan 7 vs Everton (a) 0-1
Att: 29,406

LEAGUE CUP COMPETITION

1970/71 SEASON
2nd Round
Sep 8 vs Halifax Town (h) 3-1
Att: 20,029 Durban 2, Hector
3rd Round
Oct 7 vs Millwall (h) 4-2
Att: 25,537 Hinton (pen), McGovern, Mackay, O'Hare
4th Round
Oct 27 vs Coventry City (a) 0-1
Att: 26,557

1971/72 SEASON
2nd Round
Sep 8 vs Leeds United (h) 0-0
Att: 36,023
Replay
Sep 27 vs Leeds United (a) 0-2
Att: 29,132

1972/73 SEASON
2nd Round
Sep 5 vs Swindon Town (a) 1-0
Att: 15,730 Hennessey
3rd Round
Oct 4 vs Chelsea (h) 0-0
Att: 28,065
Replay
Oct 9 vs Chelsea (a) 2-3
Att: 26,395 Hinton, McGovern

1973/74 SEASON
2nd Round
Oct 8 vs Sunderland (h) 2-2
Att: 29,172 Nish, Davies
Replay
Oct 29 vs Sunderland (a) 1-1 (aet.)
Att: 38,975 Gemmill
2nd Replay
Oct 31 vs Sunderland (a) 0-3
Att: 38,460

1974/75 SEASON
2nd Round
Sep 11 vs Portsmouth (a) 5-1
Att: 13,582 Hector 2, Lee, Rioch, Roberts (og)
3rd Round
Oct 8 vs Southampton (a) 0-5
Att: 14,911

1975/76 SEASON
2nd Round
Sep 10 vs Huddersfield Town (h) 2-1
Att: 20,602 Rioch, George
3rd Round
Oct 7 vs Middlesbrough (a) 0-1
Att: 25,694

1976/77 SEASON
2nd Round
Aug 31 vs Doncaster Rovers (a) 2-1
Att: 14,888 George, Rioch
3rd Round
Sep 22 vs Notts County (h) 1-1
Att: 24,881 George (pen)
Replay
Oct 4 vs Notts County (a) 2-1
Att: 16,276 Rioch 2
4th Round
Oct 26 vs Brighton & Hove Albion (a) 1-1
Att: 33,500 James
Replay
Nov 8 vs Brighton & Hove Albion (h) 2-1
Att: 25,880 Todd, Hector
5th Round
Dec 1 vs Bolton Wanderers (h) 1-2
Att: 25,734 George (pen)

1977/78 SEASON
2nd Round
Aug 31 vs Orient (h) 3-1
Att: 16,948 Hector, Daly (pen), Hales
3rd Round
Oct 26 vs Liverpool (a) 0-2
Att: 30,400

1978/79 SEASON
2nd Round
Aug 30 vs Leicester City (a) 1-0
Att: 16,827 Hill
3rd Round
Oct 3 vs Southampton (a) 0-1
Att: 19,109

1979/80 SEASON
2nd Round (1st leg)
Aug 29 vs Middlesbrough (h) 0-1
Att: 15,205

2nd Round (2nd leg)
Sep 4 vs Middlesbrough (a) 1-1 (agg. 1-2)
Att: 19,463 Crawford

1980/81 SEASON
2nd Round (1st leg)
Aug 26 vs Queen's Park Rangers (a) 0-0
Att: 11,244

2nd Round (2nd leg)
Sep 3 vs Queen's Park Rangers (h) 0-0 (aet.)
Att: 16,728 Q.P.R. won 5-3 on penalties

1981/82 SEASON
2nd Round (1st leg)
Oct 7 vs West Ham United (h) 2-3
Att: 13,764 Hector, Stewart (og)

2nd Round (2nd leg)
Oct 27 vs West Ham Utd. (a) 0-2 (agg. 2-5)
Att: 21,043

1982/83 SEASON
1st Round (1st leg)
Aug 31 vs Halifax Town (a) 1-2
Att: 2,820 Swindlehurst

1st Round (2nd leg)
Sep 15 vs Halifax Town (h) 5-2 (agg. 6-4)
Att: 8,534 Skivington, Hill, Buckley 2 (1 pen), Wilson

2nd Round (1st leg)
Oct 6 vs Hartlepool United (h) 2-0
Att: 7,656 Watson (og), Swindlehurst

2nd Round (2nd leg)
Oct 12 vs Hartlepool U. (a) 2-4 (aet) (agg 4-4)
Att: 3,596 Wilson, Brolly
Derby County won on Away Goals

3rd Round
Nov 9 vs Birmingham City (a) 1-3
Att: 12,475 Swindlehurst

1983/84 SEASON
2nd Round (1st leg)
Oct 5 vs Birmingham City (h) 0-3
Att: 13,114

2nd Round (2nd leg)
Oct 25 vs Birmingham C. (a) 0-4 (agg. 0-7)
Att: 7,786

1984/85 SEASON
1st Round (1st leg)
Aug 29 vs Hartlepool United (h) 5-1
Att: 9,281 Wilson 4, Powell

1st Round (2nd leg)
Sep 5 vs Hartlepool United (a) 1-0 (agg. 6-1)
Att: 1,862 Robertson (pen)

1985/86 SEASON
1st Round (1st leg)
Aug 21 vs Hartlepool United (h) 3-0
Att: 8,415 Davison 2, McClaren

1st Round (2nd leg)
Sep 4 vs Hartlepool United (a) 0-2 (agg. 3-2)
Att: 1,611

2nd Round (1st leg)
Sep 25 vs Leicester City (h) 2-0
Att: 12,504 MacLaren (pen), Chandler

2nd Round (2nd leg)
Oct 7 vs Leicester City (a) 1-1 (agg. 3-1)
Att: 10,373 Davison

3rd Round
Oct 30 vs Nottingham Forest (h) 1-2
Att: 25,000 Chandler (pen)

1986/87 SEASON
1st Round (1st leg)
Aug 27 vs Chester (h) 0-1
Att: 8,531

1st Round (2nd leg)
Sep 3 vs Chester (a) 2-1 (aet.) (agg. 2-2)
Att: 4,012 Gee, Davison
Derby County won on Away Goals

2nd Round (1st leg)
Sep 24 vs West Bromwich Albion (h) 4-1
Att: 11,304 Chandler, Davison 2, Micklewhite

2nd Round (2nd leg)
Oct 7 vs West Brom. Alb. (a) 1-0 (agg. 5-1)
Att: 6,765 Gee

3rd Round
Oct 29 vs Aston Villa (h) 1-1
Att: 19,374 Harbey

16

Replay
Nov 4 vs Aston Villa (a) 1-2
Att: 19,477 Williams

1987/88 SEASON
2nd Round (1st leg)
Sep 22 vs Southend United (a) 0-1
Att: 4,605

2nd Round (2nd leg)
Oct 7 vs Southend United (h) 0-0 (agg. 0-1)
Att: 12,118

1988/89 SEASON
2nd Round (1st leg)
Sep 28 vs Southend United (h) 1-0
Att: 9,703 Hebberd

2nd Round (2nd leg)
Oct 11 vs Southend Utd. (a) 2-1 (agg. 3-1)
Att: 4,422 Penney, Hebberd

3rd Round
Nov 1 vs West Ham United (a) 0-5
Att: 14,226

1989/90 SEASON
2nd Round (1st leg)
Sep 19 vs Cambridge United (a) 1-2
Att: 5,333 Goddard

2nd Round (2nd leg)
Oct 4 vs Cambridge Utd. (h) 5-0 (agg. 6-2)
Att: 12,525 Saunders 3, Goddard, McMinn

3rd Round
Oct 25 vs Sheffield Wednesday (h) 2-1
Att: 18,042 Saunders 2 (1 pen)

4th Round
Nov 22 vs West Bromwich Albion (h) 2-0
Att: 21,313 McMinn 2

5th Round
Jan 17 vs West Ham United (a) 1-1
Att: 25,035 Saunders

Replay
Jan 24 vs West Ham United (h) 0-0 (aet.)
Att: 22,510

2nd Replay
Jan 31 vs West Ham United (a) 1-2
Att: 25,166 Saunders

1990/91 SEASON
2nd Round (1st leg)
Sep 25 vs Carlisle United (a) 1-1
Att: 7,628 Saunders

2nd Round (2nd leg)
Oct 10 vs Carlisle United (h) 1-0 (agg. 2-1)
Att: 12,253 Saunders

3rd Round
Oct 31 vs Sunderland (h) 6-0
Att: 16,422 Harford 3, Bennett (og), Ramage 2

4th Round
Nov 28 vs Sheffield Wednesday (a) 1-1
Att: 25,649 Saunders

Replay
Dec 12 vs Sheffield Wednesday (h) 1-2
Att: 17,050 Micklewhite

1991/92 SEASON
2nd Round (1st leg)
Sep 25 vs Ipswich Town (h) 0-0
Att: 10,215

2nd Round (2nd leg)
Oct 8 vs Ipswich Town (a) 2-0 (agg. 2-0)
Att: 8,982 Gee, Williams P (pen)

3rd Round
Oct 29 vs Oldham Athletic (a) 1-2
Att: 11,219 Forsyth

1992/93 SEASON
2nd Round (1st leg)
Sep 23 vs Southend United (a) 0-1
Att: 2,492

2nd Round (2nd leg)
Oct 7 vs Southend United (h) 7-0 (agg. 7-1)
Att: 13,328 Kitson, Martin (og), Gabbiadini 2, Simpson 2, Johnson

3rd Round
Oct 28 vs Arsenal (h) 1-1
Att: 22,208 Simpson (pen)

Replay
Dec 1 vs Arsenal (a) 1-2
Att: 24,587 Pembridge (pen)

1993/94 SEASON
2nd Round (1st leg)
Sep 22 vs Exeter City (a) 3-1
Att: 5,634 Kitson, Simpson, Gabbiadini

2nd Round (2nd leg)
Oct 6 vs Exeter City (h) 2-0 (aggregate 5-1)
Att: 10,659 Gabbiadini, Johnson

3rd Round
Oct 27 vs Tottenham Hotspur (h) 0-1
Att: 19,855

1994/95 SEASON
2nd Round (1st leg)
Sep 20 vs Reading (a) 1-3
Att: 6,056 Gabbiadini

2nd Round (2nd leg)
Sep 28 vs Reading (h) 2-0 (aet.) (agg. 3-3)
Att: 9,476 Gabbiadini, Williams
Derby County won on Away Goals

3rd Round
Oct 26 vs Portsmouth (a) 1-0
Att: 8,568 Simpson

4th Round
Nov 30 vs Swindon Town (a) 1-2
Att: 8,920 Stallard

EUROPEAN CUP COMPETITION
1972/73 SEASON
1st Round (1st leg)
Sep 13 vs Zeljeznicar Sarajevo (h) 2-0
Att: 27,350 McFarland, Gemmill

1st Round (2nd leg)
Sep 27 vs Zeljez. Sarajevo (a) 2-1 (agg 4-1)
Att: 60,000 Hinton, O'Hare

2nd Round (1st leg)
Oct 25 vs Benfica (h) 3-0
Att: 38,100 McFarland, Hector, McGovern

2nd Round (2nd leg)
Nov 8 vs Benfica (a) 0-0 (aggregate 3-0)
Att: 75,000

Quarter-Final (1st leg)
Mar 7 vs Spartak Trnava (a) 0-1
Att: 28,000

Quarter-Final (2nd leg)
Mar 21 vs Spartak Trnava (h) 2-0 (agg. 2-1)
Att: 36,472 Hector 2

Semi-Final (1st leg)
Apr 11 vs Juventus (a) 1-3
Att: 72,000 Hector

Semi-Final (2nd leg)
Apr 25 vs Juventus (h) 0-0 (aggregate 1-3)
Att: 35,350

1975/76 SEASON
1st Round (1st leg)
Sep 17 vs Slovan Bratislava (a) 0-1
Att: 45,000

1st Round (2nd leg)
Oct 1 vs Slov. Bratislava (h) 3-0 (agg. 3-1)
Att: 30,888 Bourne, Lee 2

2nd Round (1st leg)
Oct 22 vs Real Madrid (h) 4-1
Att: 34,839 George 3 (2 pens), Nish

2nd Round (2nd leg)
Nov 5 vs Real Madrid (a) 1-5 (aet) (agg 5-6)
Att: 120,000 George

UEFA CUP COMPETITION
1974/75 SEASON
1st Round (1st leg)
Sep 18 vs Servette (h) 4-1
Att: 17,716 Hector 2, Daniel, Lee

1st Round (2nd leg)
Oct 2 vs Servette (a) 2-1 (aggregate 6-2)
Att: 9,600 Lee, Hector

2nd Round (1st leg)
Oct 23 vs Atletico Madrid (h) 2-2
Att: 29,347 Nish, Rioch (pen)

2nd Round (2nd leg)
Nov 6 vs Atl. Madrid (a) 2-2 (aet) (agg 4-4)
Att: 35,000 Rioch, Hector
Derby County won 7-6 on penalties

3rd Round (1st leg)
Nov 27 vs Velez Mostar (h) 3-1
Att: 26,131 Bourne 2, Hinton

3rd Round (2nd leg)
Dec 11 vs Velez Mostar (a) 1-4 (agg. 4-5)
Att: 15,000 Hector

1976/77 SEASON
1st Round (1st leg)
Sep 15 vs Finn Harps (h) 12-0
Att: 13,353 Hector 5, James 3, George 3, Rioch

1st Round (2nd leg)
Sep 29 vs Finn Harps (a) 4-1 (agg. 16-1)
Att: 2,217 Hector 2, George 2

2nd Round (1st leg)
Oct 20 vs AEK Athens (a) 0-2
Att: 32,000

2nd Round (2nd leg)
Nov 3 vs AEK Athens (h) 2-3 (agg. 2-5)
Att: 28,000

1970-71

1	Aug	15	(a)	Chelsea	L	1-2	O'Hare	46,969
2		19	(a)	Wolves	W	4-2	McGovern 2, Durban, O'Hare	29,910
3		22	(h)	Stoke C	W	2-0	Hinton (pen), Wignall	35,461
4		26	(h)	Ipswich T	W	2-0	Hector, Harper (og)	30,869
5		29	(a)	Huddersfield T	D	0-0		27,997
6	Sep	2	(h)	Coventry C	L	3-4	McGovern, Hector, Hinton	31,621
7		5	(h)	Newcastle U	L	1-2	O'Hare	30,466
8		12	(a)	Southampton	L	0-4		19,429
9		19	(h)	Burnley	W	1-0	Hinton	26,749
10		26	(a)	West Brom A	L	1-2	O'Hare	31,216
11	Oct	3	(h)	Tottenham H	D	1-1	Hinton (pen)	36,007
12		10	(a)	Everton	D	1-1	McGovern	46,614
13		17	(h)	Chelsea	L	1-2	O'Hare	35,166
14		24	(h)	Leeds U	L	0-2		32,797
15		31	(a)	Arsenal	L	0-2		43,013
16	Nov	7	(h)	Liverpool	D	0-0		33,004
17		14	(a)	Manchester C	D	1-1	O'Hare	31,817
18		21	(h)	Blackpool	W	2-0	McFarland, Hector	28,237
19		28	(a)	Nottingham F	W	4-2	McGovern, O'Hare, Wignall, Gemmill	30,539
20	Dec	5	(h)	West Ham U	L	2-4	Durban, Wignall	30,806
21		12	(a)	Crystal P	D	0-0		24,218
22		19	(a)	Stoke C	L	0-1		21,906
23		26	(h)	Manchester U	D	4-4	Mackay, Hector, Wignall, Gemmill	34,068
24	Jan	9	(h)	Wolves	L	1-2	Gemmill (pen)	34,243
25		16	(a)	Ipswich T	W	1-0	O'Hare	20,332
26	Feb	6	(a)	West Ham U	W	4-1	Hector 2, Hinton 2	26,606
27		17	(h)	Crystal P	W	1-0	Mackay	23,521
28		20	(a)	Blackpool	W	1-0	O'Hare	17,892
29		27	(h)	Arsenal	W	2-0	McFarland, Hector	35,775
30	Mar	6	(a)	Leeds U	L	0-1		36,467
31		12	(h)	Manchester C	D	0-0		31,987
32		20	(a)	Liverpool	L	0-2		40,940
33		27	(a)	Newcastle U	L	1-3	Hector	26,052
34		31	(h)	Nottingham F	L	1-2	Hector	34,857
35	Apr	3	(h)	Huddersfield T	W	3-2	Hinton 2 (1 pen), Hector	24,194
36		7	(a)	Tottenham H	L	1-2	Hinton	25,627
37		10	(a)	Manchester U	W	2-1	O'Hare 2	44,203
38		12	(h)	Southampton	D	0-0		26,420
39		17	(h)	Everton	W	3-1	O'Hare 2, Hector	28,973
40		24	(a)	Burnley	W	2-1	McGovern, Durban	10,373
41		27	(a)	Coventry C	D	0-0		22,051
42	May	1	(h)	West Brom A	W	2-0	Hinton, Durban	33,661

FINAL LEAGUE POSITION : 9th in Division One

Appearances

Sub. Appearances

Goals

Green	Webster	Robson	Durban	McFarland	Mackay	McGovern	Carlin	O'Hare	Hector	Hinton	Wignall	Hennessey	Rhodes	Richardson	Walker	Gemmill	Daniel	Bulin	Boulton	Todd	Bourne		
1	2	3	4	5	6	7	8	9	10	11*	12												1
1	2	3	4*	5	6	7	8	9	10	11	12												2
1	2	3		5	6	7	8	9	10	11	12	4*											3
1	2	3	4*	5	6	7	8	9	10	11	12												4
1	2	3		5	6	4	8	9	10	11	7												5
1	2	3		5	6	7	8	9	10	11	4												6
1	2	3	4	5	6	7	8	9	10*	11	12												7
1	2	3	4*		6	7	8	9	10	11	12	5											8
1		3	4*		6		8	9	10	11	12	5	2	7									9
1		3	4		6		8	9	10	11		5	2			7							10
1	2	3	4*		6	12	8	9	10	11						7	5						11
1	2	3		5	6	4	8	9	10	11						7							12
1	2	3			6	4	8	9	10	11						7	5						13
1	2	3		5	6		8	9	10	11		4				7							14
1	2	3	8	5	6			9	10	11		4				7							15
1	2	3	4	5	6		8	9	10	11						7							16
1	2	3		5	6	7		9	10	11		4				8							17
1	2	3	8	5	6			9	10	11		4				7							18
1	2	3	4		6	7		9	10		8	5				11							19
1	2	3	4		6	7		9	10		8	5				11							20
1	2	3	7	5	6			9	10		8	4*				11	12						21
1	2	3	7	5	6	12		9	10			4				11		8*					22
1	2		7	5	6			9	10		8	4				11	3						23
	2	12		5	6*	7		9	10		8	4				11	3		1				24
	2	3	8	5	6	7		9	10			4				11			1				25
	2	3	4	5	6	7		9	10	11						8			1				26
	2	3	4	5	6	7		9	10	11						8			1				27
	2	3	4	5	6	7		9	10	11						8			1				28
	2			5	6	7		9	10	11				3		8			1	4			29
	2	3		5	6	7		9	10	11						8			1	4			30
	2			5	6	7		9	10	11				3		8			1	4			31
	2		12	5	6	7		9*	10	11				3		8			1	4			32
	2	3	12	5	6	7*		9	10		8	.				11			1	4			33
	2			5	6			9	10	11	8			3		7			1	4			34
	2			5	6			9	10	11	8			3		7			1	4			35
	2			5	6	7		9	10	11				3		8			1	4			36
		3	4	5	6	7		9	10	11						8			1	2			37
		3	4	5	6	7		9	10	11						8			1	2			38
		3	4	5	6	7		9	10	11						8			1	2			39
		3	4	5	6	7		9	10	11									1	2	8		40
	12	3	4	5	6	7		9	10	11									1	2	8*		41
		3	4	5	6	7		9	10	11						8			1	2			42
23	34	34	26	35	42	32	13	42	42	34	10	12	3	8	1	31	4	1	19	14	2		
	1	1	2		2						7						1						
			4	2	2	6		13	11	10	4					3							

1971-72

1	Aug	14	(h)	Manchester U	D	2-2	Wignall, Hector	35,386
2		18	(h)	West Ham U	W	2-0	Wignall, O'Hare	30,783
3		21	(a)	Leicester C	W	2-0	Hector, Hinton (pen)	35,460
4		24	(a)	Coventry C	D	2-2	Wignall, O'Hare	27,759
5		28	(h)	Southampton	D	2-2	McGovern, Hector	28,498
6		31	(a)	Ipswich T	D	0-0		18,687
7	Sep	4	(a)	Everton	W	2-0	Wignall, Hector	41,024
8		11	(h)	Stoke C	W	4-0	Todd, Gemmill, O'Hare, Hinton	32,545
9		18	(a)	Chelsea	D	1-1	McFarland	42,872
10		25	(h)	West Brom A	D	0-0		30,628
11	Oct	2	(a)	Newcastle U	W	1-0	Hinton	32,077
12		9	(h)	Tottenham H	D	2-2	Todd, McFarland	35,744
13		16	(a)	Manchester U	L	0-1		53,247
14		23	(h)	Arsenal	W	2-1	O'Hare, Hinton (pen)	36,480
15		30	(a)	Nottingham F	W	2-0	Robson, Hinton (pen)	37,170
16	Nov	6	(h)	Crystal P	W	3-0	Wignall, Hector, Bell (og)	30,388
17		13	(a)	Wolves	L	1-2	O'Hare	32,957
18		20	(h)	Sheffield U	W	3-0	Hinton 2 (2 pens), Hector	35,326
19		27	(a)	Huddersfield T	L	1-2	McGovern	15,329
20	Dec	4	(h)	Manchester C	W	3-1	Webster, Durban, Hinton (pen)	35,384
21		11	(a)	Liverpool	L	2-3	O'Hare 2	44,601
22		18	(h)	Everton	W	2-0	Hinton 2	27,895
23		27	(a)	Leeds U	L	0-3		44,214
24	Jan	1	(h)	Chelsea	W	1-0	Gemmill	33,063
25		8	(a)	Southampton	W	2-1	O'Hare, Durban	19,321
26		22	(a)	West Ham U	D	3-3	Hector, Hinton, Durban	31,045
27		29	(h)	Coventry C	W	1-0	Robson	29,385
28	Feb	12	(a)	Arsenal	L	0-2		52,055
29		19	(h)	Nottingham F	W	4-0	Hinton 2, Hector, O'Hare	31,801
30	Mar	4	(h)	Wolves	W	2-1	Hinton (pen), McFarland	33,456
31		11	(a)	Tottenham H	W	1-0	Hinton (pen)	36,310
32		18	(h)	Leicester C	W	3-0	O'Hare, Hector, Durban	34,019
33		22	(h)	Ipswich T	W	1-0	Hector	26,738
34		25	(a)	Stoke C	D	1-1	Durban	33,771
35		28	(a)	Crystal P	W	1-0	Walker	21,185
36	Apr	1	(h)	Leeds U	W	2-0	O'Hare, Hunter (og)	38,611
37		3	(h)	Newcastle U	L	0-1		38,119
38		5	(a)	West Brom A	D	0-0		32,439
39		8	(a)	Sheffield U	W	4-0	Gemmill, O'Hare, Hector, Durban	38,238
40		15	(h)	Huddersfield T	W	3-0	McFarland, O'Hare, Hector	31,414
41		22	(a)	Manchester C	L	0-2		55,023
42	May	1	(h)	Liverpool	W	1-0	McGovern	39,159

FINAL LEAGUE POSITION : 1st in Division One

Appearances

Sub. Appearances

Goals

Boulton	Webster	Robson	McGovern	Hennessey	Todd	Gemmill	Wignall	O'Hare	Hector	Hinton	McFarland	Durban	Powell	Walker	Bailey	
1	2	3	4	5	6	7	8	9	10	11						1
1	2	3	4	5	6	7	8	9	10	11						2
1	2	3	4	5	6	7	8	9	10	11						3
1	2	3	4		6	7	8	9	10	11	5					4
1		3	6	4	2	7		9	10	11	5	8				5
1		3	6	4	2	7	9		10	11	5	8				6
1	2	3	6		4	7	9		10	11	5	8				7
1	2	3		4	6	8		9	10	11	5	7				8
1	2	3	6		4	7	8	9	10	11	5					9
1	2	3	12		4	6	8	9	10	11	5	7*				10
1	2	3	7	4	6			9	10	11	5	8				11
1	2*	3	6		4	7	12	9	10	11	5	8				12
1		3	6	4	2	7		9	10	11	5	8				13
1	2*	3	6		4	7		9	10	11	5	8	12			14
1	2	3	7		6	8		9	10	11	5		4			15
1	2	3	6	5	4		8	9	10	11		7				16
1	2	3	7	6	4	8		9	10	11	5					17
1	2	3	7	6	4	8		9	10	11	5					18
1	2	3	7	6	4	8		9	10	11	5					19
1	2	3	6		4	8		9	10	11	5	7				20
1	3		6	4	2*	8		9	10	11	5	7	12			21
1	2	3	6	4		8		9	10	11	5	7				22
1	2	3	7	6		8		9	10	11	5			4		23
1	2	3	6		4	8		9	10	11	5	7				24
1	2	3	7		6	8		9	10	11	5	4				25
1	2	3	7		6	8		9	10	11	5	4				26
1	2	3	7		6	8		9	10	11	5	4				27
1	2	3	7		6	8		9	10	11	5	4				28
1	2	3	7		6	8		9	10	11	5	4				29
1	2	3	7		6	8		9	10	11	5	4				30
1	2	3	7	4	6	8		9	10	11	5					31
1	2	3	7	8*	6	11		9	10		5	4	12			32
1	2	3	7		6	8		9	10	11*	5	4	12			33
1	2	3	7		6	8		9	10		5	4	11			34
1	2	3		7	6	8		9	10		5	4	11			35
1	2	3	7		6	8		9	10		5	4	11			36
1	2	3	7		6	8		9	10	11	5	4				37
1	2	3	7		6	8		9	10	11	5	4				38
1	2	3	7		6	8		9	10	11	5	4				39
1	2	3	7		6	8		9	10	11	5	4				40
1	2*	3	7	12	6	8		9	10	11	5	4				41
1		3	7		6	8		9	10	11	5	4	2			42
42	38	41	39	17	40	40	10	40	42	38	38	31	2	3	1	
			1	1			1						1	3		
	1	2	3		2	3	5	13	12	15	4	6		1		

21

1972-73

1	Aug	12	(a)	Southampton	D	1-1	Hinton	20,525
2		15	(a)	Crystal P	D	0-0		23,401
3		19	(h)	Chelsea	L	1-2	Hector	31,868
4		23	(h)	Manchester C	W	1-0	Walker	31,173
5		26	(a)	Norwich C	L	0-1		29,847
6		29	(a)	Everton	L	0-1		39,780
7	Sep	2	(h)	Liverpool	W	2-1	O'Hare, Hinton	32,524
8		9	(a)	West Brom A	L	1-2	McFarland	17,262
9		16	(h)	Birmingham C	W	1-0	Hector	33,753
10		23	(a)	Manchester U	L	0-3		48,255
11		30	(h)	Tottenham H	W	2-1	Hector, Hinton (pen)	32,133
12	Oct	7	(a)	Leeds U	L	0-5		36,477
13		14	(h)	Leicester C	W	2-1	Hinton (pen), Hennessey	31,841
14		21	(a)	Ipswich T	L	1-3	Hinton (pen)	16,948
15		28	(h)	Sheffield U	W	2-1	Todd, O'Hare	30,929
16	Nov	4	(a)	Manchester C	L	0-4		35,829
17		11	(h)	Crystal P	D	2-2	Hinton, Powell	26,716
18		18	(a)	West Ham U	W	2-1	Hector 2	28,154
19		25	(h)	Arsenal	W	5-0	McFarland, McGovern, Hector, Hinton, Davies	31,034
20	Dec	2	(a)	Wolves	W	2-1	Hector, Hennessey	24,891
21		9	(h)	Coventry C	W	2-0	Gemmill, Hinton (pen)	31,002
22		16	(h)	Newcastle U	D	1-1	Hector	28,826
23		23	(a)	Stoke C	L	0-4		25,098
24		26	(h)	Manchester U	W	3-1	McFarland 2, Hinton	35,098
25		30	(a)	Chelsea	D	1-1	O'Hare	29,794
26	Jan	6	(h)	Norwich C	W	1-0	Hinton (pen)	27,580
27		20	(a)	Liverpool	D	1-1	Davies	45,996
28		27	(h)	West Brom A	W	2-0	Hinton (pen), Davies	28,833
29	Feb	10	(a)	Birmingham C	L	0-2		38,096
30		14	(h)	Stoke C	L	0-3		22,106
31		17	(h)	Southampton	W	4-0	Hector 2, Hinton, McCarthy (og)	26,426
32		28	(a)	Newcastle U	L	0-2		34,286
33	Mar	3	(h)	Leeds U	L	2-3	Durban, Hector	38,462
34		10	(a)	Leicester C	D	0-0		29,690
35		24	(a)	Sheffield U	L	1-3	Davies	24,403
36		31	(a)	Arsenal	W	1-0	Powell	45,217
37	Apr	14	(a)	Coventry C	W	2-0	O'Hare, Hector	22,762
38		18	(a)	Tottenham H	L	0-1		22,695
39		21	(h)	West Ham U	D	1-1	Gemmill (pen)	28,727
40		28	(h)	Everton	W	3-1	Gemmill (pen), Hinton, Nish	24,094
41		30	(h)	Ipswich T	W	3-0	Hector 2, Davies	20,347
42	May	4	(h)	Wolves	W	3-0	Davies 2, McFarland	31,590

FINAL LEAGUE POSITION : 7th in Division One

Appearances

Sub. Appearances

Goals

Boulton	Webster	Robson	Durban	McFarland	Todd	McGovern	Gemmill	O'Hare	Hector	Hinton	Hennessey	Walker	Powell	Lewis	Nish	Daniel	Davies	Butlin	Sims	Parry	Moseley	No.
1	2	3	4	5	6	7	8	9	10	11												1
1	2	3	4		6	7	8	9	10	11	5											2
1	2	3	4	5	6	7	8	9	10			11										3
1				5	6	7	8	9	10		4	11	2	3								4
1			12	5	6	7	8	9	10		4*	11	2		3							5
1				5	6	7	8	9	10		4	11	2		3							6
1				5	6	7	8	9	10	11	4		2		3							7
1				5	6	7	8	9	10	11	4		2		3							8
1				5	6	7	8	9	10	11	4		2		3							9
1				5	6	7	8	9	10	11	4		2		3							10
1	2		12	5	6	7	8	9	10	11	4*				3							11
1	2		4	5	6		8	9	10	11					3	7						12
1	2			5	6	7		9	10	11	4		8		3							13
1	2		11	5	6	7			10	9	4		8		3							14
1	3			5	6	7		9	10	11	4		2		8							15
1	3		12	5	6	7				11*	4		2		8		9	10				16
1	2	3		5	6	7		9	10	11	4				8							17
1	2			5	6	7	8	9	10	11	4				3							18
1	2			5	6	7	8		10	11	4				3		9					19
1	2				6	7	8	9	10	11	4				3	5						20
1	2				6	7	8	4	10	11					3	5	9					21
1	2			5	6	7	8	4	10						3*		9		12			22
1	2			5	6	7	8	9	10	11	4				3							23
1	2			5	6	7	8		10	11	4				3		9					24
1	2			5	6	7		8	10	11	4				3		9					25
1				5	6	7	8	4	10	11			2		3		9					26
1	2			5	6	7		8	10		4	11			3		9					27
1	2			5	6	7	8		10	11	4				3		9					28
1	2		4	5	6	7	11		10						3		9		8	6		29
1	2		4				8		10	11*					3	5	9		7	12		30
1	2			5	6	7	8	4	10	11					3		9					31
1	2*		12	5	6	7	8	4	10	11					3		9					32
1			11	5	6	7	8	4	10				2		3		9					33
1	2*		12	5	6	7	8	4	10	11					3		9					34
1	2		11	5	6	7*	8	9	10		4				3		12					35
1	2			5	6	7		8	10	11					3		9			4		36
1	2		4*	5	6	7	8	9	10	11					3					12		37
	2		12	5	6	7*	8	9	10	11					3					4	1	38
			12	5	6	7	8	9	10	11			2		3					4*	1	39
1	2		7	5	6		8		10	11	4				3		9					40
1	2			5	6	7	8	4	10	11					3		9					41
1	2			5	6	7	8	4	10	11					3		9					42
40	26	10	11	38	41	39	34	34	41	37	21	5	22	2	34	9	19	1	2	4	2	
			7														1		1	2		
			1	5	1	1	3	4	14	13	2	1	2		1		7					

1973-74

#		Date			Opponent	Result		Scorers	Attendance
1	Aug	25	(h)	Chelsea	W	1-0	McGovern	31,847
2		29	(h)	Manchester C	W	1-0	Hinton	31,295
3	Sep	1	(a)	Birmingham C	D	0-0		34,899
4		4	(a)	Liverpool	L	0-2		45,237
5		8	(h)	Everton	W	2-1	Davies, Hector	27,638
6		12	(h)	Liverpool	W	3-1	McFarland, Davies, Hector	32,867
7		15	(a)	Burnley	D	1-1	Davies	24,493
8		18	(a)	Coventry C	L	0-1		26,511
9		22	(h)	Southampton	W	6-2	Hector 3, Davies 2, Hinton (pen)	25,500
10		29	(a)	Tottenham H	L	0-1		31,408
11	Oct	6	(h)	Norwich C	D	1-1	Davies	25,984
12		13	(a)	Manchester U	W	1-0	Hector	43,724
13		20	(h)	Leicester C	W	2-1	McGovern, Hector	32,203
14		27	(a)	West Ham U	D	0-0		31,237
15	Nov	3	(h)	Queen's Park R	L	1-2	Gemmill (pen)	28,092
16		10	(a)	Ipswich T	L	0-3		23,551
17		17	(a)	Sheffield U	L	0-3		25,438
18		24	(h)	Leeds U	D	0-0		36,003
19	Dec	8	(h)	Arsenal	D	1-1	McFarland	25,161
20		15	(a)	Newcastle U	W	2-0	Davies, Hinton	19,470
21		22	(h)	Tottenham H	W	2-0	Hinton 2	23,672
22		26	(a)	Stoke C	D	0-0		24,045
23		29	(a)	Everton	L	1-2	Hector	37,429
24	Jan	1	(h)	Birmingham C	D	1-1	Bourne	31,189
25		12	(h)	Burnley	W	5-1	Hector 3, Bourne 2	24,948
26		19	(a)	Chelsea	D	1-1	Bourne	27,185
27	Feb	2	(h)	Newcastle U	W	1-0	McFarland	24,992
28		6	(a)	Manchester C	L	0-1		22,845
29		16	(h)	Manchester U	D	2-2	Nish, Hector	29,987
30		23	(a)	Norwich C	W	4-2	Bourne 2, Davies, Hector	25,175
31	Mar	2	(h)	Stoke C	D	1-1	Bourne	28,676
32		5	(a)	Southampton	D	1-1	Newton	17,191
33		9	(h)	West Ham U	D	1-1	Rioch (pen)	24,683
34		16	(a)	Leicester C	W	1-0	McFarland	30,423
35		23	(h)	Ipswich T	W	2-0	Hector, Rioch (pen)	23,860
36		30	(a)	Queen's Park R	D	0-0		19,795
37	Apr	6	(a)	Leeds U	L	0-2		37,838
38		9	(a)	Wolves	L	0-4		23,546
39		13	(h)	Sheffield U	W	4-1	Hector 3, Davies	25,029
40		15	(h)	Coventry C	W	1-0	Hector	23,348
41		20	(a)	Arsenal	L	0-2		26,017
42		27	(h)	Wolves	W	2-0	Powell, Hector	26,571

FINAL LEAGUE POSITION : 3rd in Division One

Appearances

Sub. Appearances

Goals

	Boulton	Webster	Nish	Powell	McFarland	Todd	McGovern	Gemmill	Davies	Hector	Hinton	O'Hare	Newton	Daniel	Walker	Thomas	Bourne	Rioch	
1	1	2	3	4	5	6	7	8	9	10	11								1
2	1	2	3	4	5	6	7	8	9	10	11								2
3	1	2	3	4	5	6	7	8		10	11	9							3
4	1	2	3	4	5	6	7	8		10	11	9							4
5	1	2	3	4	5	6	7	8	9	10	11								5
6	1	2	3	4	5	6	7	8	9	10	11								6
7	1	2	3	4	5	6	7	8	9	10	11								7
8	1	2	3	4*	5	6	7	8	9	10	11	12							8
9	1	2	3	4	5	6	7	8	9	10	11								9
10	1	2	3	4	5	6	7	11		10		9	8						10
11	1	2	3	4		6		8	9	10	11		7	5					11
12	1	2	3		5	6	7	8	9	10	11		4						12
13	1	2	3		5	6	7	8	9	10	11		4						13
14	1	2	3		5	6	7	8	9	10	11		4						14
15	1		3		5	6	7	8	9	10	11		4	2					15
16	1	2	3		5	6	7	8		10	11	9	4						16
17	1		3		5	6	7	8		10	11	9	4	2					17
18	1	2	3		5	6	7	8	12	10	11	9*	4						18
19	1	2	3		5	6	7	8	9	10	11		4						19
20	1	2	3		5	6	7	8	9	10	11		4						20
21	1	2	3		5	6	7	8	9	10	11		4						21
22	1	2	3		5	6	7	8	9*	10	11		4		12				22
23	1	2		12	5	6	7	8		10	11	9*	4	3					23
24	1	2			5	6	7	8		10	11		4	3			9		24
25	1	2	3	4	5	6	7	8		10	11						9		25
26	1	2	3	7	5	6		8		10	11		4				9		26
27	1	2	3	7	5	6	11		9	10			4				8		27
28	1	2	3	7	5		11		9	10	12		4			6	8*		28
29	1	2	3	7	5			8	9	10			4			6	11		29
30	1	2	3	7	5	6		8	9	10							11	4	30
31	1	2	3	7	5	6		8	9	10							11	4	31
32	1	2	3	7	5	6			9*	10	12		8				11	4	32
33	1	2	3	7	5	6			9*	10	12		8				11	4	33
34	1	2	3	7	5	6		8	9	10							11	4	34
35	1		3	7	5	6		8	9	10						2	11	4	35
36	1	2	3	7		6		8	9	10				5			11	4	36
37	1	2	3	7		6		8	9	10	12			5			11	4*	37
38	1	2	3	7		6		8	9	10				5			11	4	38
39	1	2	3	7	5	6		8	9	10							11	4	39
40	1	2	3	7	5	6		8	9	10							11	4	40
41	1	2	3	7	5	6		8	9	10							11	4	41
42	1		3	7	5	6		8	9	10						2	11	4	42
	42	38	40	29	38	40	26	38	32	42	25	7	21	8		4	19	13	
				1					1		4	1			1				
			1	1	4		2	1	9	19	5		1				7	2	

1974-75

1	Aug	17	(a)	Everton	D	0-0		42,293
2		21	(h)	Coventry C	D	1-1	Lee	25,717
3		24	(h)	Sheffield U	W	2-0	Davies, Hector	23,088
4		27	(a)	Coventry C	D	1-1	Davies	18,659
5		31	(a)	Tottenham H	L	0-2		20,670
6	Sep	7	(h)	Newcastle U	D	2-2	Davies, Lee	21,197
7		14	(a)	Birmingham C	L	2-3	Rioch, Davies	27,345
8		21	(h)	Burnley	W	3-2	Rioch (pen), Hector, Lee	21,377
9		25	(h)	Chelsea	W	4-1	Webster, Rioch, Daniel, Hector	22,036
10		28	(a)	Stoke C	D	1-1	Lee	23,590
11	Oct	5	(a)	West Ham U	D	2-2	Hector, Lee	32,938
12		12	(h)	Leicester C	W	1-0	Rioch	24,753
13		15	(a)	Sheffield U	W	2-1	Lee 2	21,882
14		19	(a)	Carlisle U	L	0-3		13,353
15		26	(h)	Middlesborough	L	2-3	Hector, Hinton	24,036
16	Nov	2	(a)	Leeds U	W	1-0	Lee	33,551
17		9	(h)	Queen's Park R	W	5-2	Hector 3, Lee, Rioch	23,339
18		16	(a)	Arsenal	L	1-3	Rioch (pen)	32,286
19		23	(h)	Ipswich T	W	2-0	Rioch, Hector	24,341
20	Dec	7	(a)	Liverpool	D	2-2	Davies, Bourne	41,058
21		14	(h)	Everton	L	0-1		24,891
22		21	(a)	Luton T	L	0-1		12,862
23		26	(h)	Birmingham C	W	2-1	Rioch, Bourne	26,121
24		28	(a)	Manchester C	W	2-1	Lee, Newton	40,188
25	Jan	11	(h)	Liverpool	W	2-0	Lee, Newton	33,463
26		18	(a)	Wolves	W	1-0	Newton	24,515
27	Feb	1	(a)	Queen's Park R	L	1-4	Rioch	20,686
28		8	(h)	Leeds U	D	0-0		33,641
29		22	(h)	Arsenal	W	2-1	Powell 2	24,002
30		25	(a)	Ipswich T	L	0-3		23,132
31	Mar	1	(h)	Tottenham H	W	3-1	Rioch, Daniel, Davies	22,995
32		8	(a)	Chelsea	W	2-1	Daniel, Hinton	22,644
33		15	(h)	Stoke C	L	1-2	Hector	29,985
34		22	(a)	Newcastle U	W	2-0	Nish, Rioch	32,201
35		29	(h)	Luton T	W	5-0	Davies 5	24,619
36		31	(a)	Burnley	W	5-2	Hector 2, Davies, Nish, Rioch	24,317
37	Apr	1	(h)	Manchester C	W	2-1	Rioch 2	32,966
38		2	(a)	Middlesborough	D	1-1	Hector	30,066
39		9	(h)	Wolves	W	1-0	Lee	30,109
40		12	(h)	West Ham U	W	1-0	Rioch	31,536
41		19	(a)	Leicester C	D	0-0		38,143
42		26	(h)	Carlisle	D	0-0		36,882

FINAL LEAGUE POSITION : 1st in Division One

Appearances

Sub. Appearances

Goals

Boulton	Webster	Nish	Rioch	Daniel	Todd	Powell	Gemmill	Davies	Hector	Lee	Bourne	Newton	Thomas	Hinton	McFarland	#
1	2	3	4	5	6	7	8	9	10*	11	12					1
1	2	3	4	5	6	7	8	9	10*	11	12					2
1	2	3	4*		6	7	8	9	10	11	12	5				3
1	2	3	4	5	6	7	8	9	10	11			5			4
1	2	3	4	5	6		8	9	10	11*	12	7				5
1	2	3	4*	5	6		8	9	10	11	12	7				6
1	2	3	4	5	6	7*	8	9	10	11		12				7
1	2	3	4	5	6		8	9	10	11		7				8
1	2	3	4	5	6		8	9	10	11		7				9
1	2	3	4*	5	6	12	8	9	10	11		7				10
1	2	3	4	5	6		8	9	10	11		7				11
1	2	3	4	5	6		8	9	10	11		7				12
1	2	3	4	5	6		8	9	10	11		7				13
1	2	3	4	5	6		8	9	10	11		7				14
1	2	3	4*	5		6	8	9	10	11		12				15
1	2	3	4	5		6	8	9	10	11						16
1	2	3	4	5		6	8*	9	10	11	12	7				17
1	2	3	4	5	6		8	9	10	11		7				18
1	2	3	4	5	6		8	9	10	11		7				19
1	2		4	5	6		8	12	10*	11	9	7	3			20
1	2		4	5	6		8	9		11	10*	7	3	12		21
1	2		4	5	6		8	9*		11	10	7	3	12		22
1	2	3	4	5	6		8	9		11	10	7				23
1	2	3	4	5	6		8	9		11	10	7				24
1		3	4	5	6		8	9	10	11		7	2			25
1		3	4	5	6		8	9	10	11		7	2			26
1		3	4	5	6		8	9	10	11*	12	7	2			27
1		3	4	5	6		8	9*	10	11	12	7	2			28
1		3	4	5	6	8			10	11	9	7	2			29
1		3	4	5	6	12	8		10	11*	9	7	2			30
1		3	4	5	6*	12	8	9	10			7	2	11		31
1		3	4	5	6		8	9	10			7	2	11		32
1		3	4	5	6		8	9	10			7	2	11		33
1		3	4	5	6		8	9	10		12	7*	2	11		34
1		3	4	5	6	7	8	9	10				2	11		35
1		3	4	5	6	7	8	9	10				2	11		36
1		3	4	5	6	7	8	9	10				2	11		37
1	3*		4	5	6		8	9	10		12	7	2	11		38
1			4	5	6		8	9	10	11		7	2		3	39
1		3	4		6		8	9*	10	11		7	2	12	5	40
1		3	4		6		8	9	10	11		7	2		5	41
1		3	4		6		8	9	10	11*		7	2	12	5	42
42	24	38	42	37	39	12	41	39	38	34	7	35	22	8	4	
						3		1			10	1		5		
	1	2	15	3		2		12	13	12	2	3		2		

27

1975-76

1	Aug	16	(a)	Sheffield U	D	1-1	George	31,316
2		19	(a)	Coventry C	D	1-1	McFarland	24,161
3		23	(h)	Queen's Park R	L	1-5	McFarland	27,950
4		27	(h)	Newcastle U	W	3-2	Lee, Hector, Craig (og)	27,585
5		30	(a)	Everton	L	0-2		32,483
6	Sep	6	(h)	Burnley	W	3-0	Gemmill, Lee, Hector	24,026
7		13	(a)	Tottenham H	W	3-2	Lee, Hector, George	28,455
8		20	(h)	Manchester C	W	1-0	Lee	28,076
9		24	(h)	Manchester U	W	2-1	George 2	33,187
10		27	(a)	Stoke C	L	0-1		25,097
11	Oct	4	(h)	Ipswich T	W	1-0	Lee	26,056
12		11	(a)	Norwich C	D	0-0		22,537
13		18	(h)	Wolves	W	3-2	Hector 2, Lee	25,861
14		25	(a)	Liverpool	D	1-1	Lee	46,324
15	Nov	1	(h)	Leeds U	W	3-2	George (pen), Gemmill, Davies	33,107
16		8	(a)	Arsenal	W	1-0	Hector	32,102
17		15	(h)	West Ham U	W	2-1	Rioch, George	31,172
18		22	(a)	Wolves	D	0-0		26,690
19		29	(h)	Middlesborough	W	3-2	Newton, Gemmill, Lee	27,745
20	Dec	6	(a)	Birmingham C	L	1-2	George	30,620
21		13	(a)	Queen's Park R	D	1-1	Rioch	25,465
22		20	(h)	Sheffield U	W	3-2	Nish, George, Garner (og)	26,455
23		26	(a)	Leicester C	L	1-2	James	26,870
24		27	(h)	Aston Villa	W	2-0	George (pen), Powell	36,230
25	Jan	10	(h)	Tottenham H	L	2-3	Powell, Davies	28,085
26		17	(a)	Burnley	W	2-1	George, James	21,088
27		31	(h)	Coventry C	W	2-0	George 2 (1 pen)	24,253
28	Feb	7	(a)	Newcastle U	L	3-4	Rioch, George, Powell	45,770
29		18	(h)	Arsenal	W	2-0	James 2	24,875
30		21	(a)	West Ham U	W	2-1	Rioch, George	24,941
31		25	(a)	Manchester U	D	1-1	Rioch	59,632
32		28	(h)	Liverpool	D	1-1	George (pen)	32,800
33	Mar	2	(a)	Leeds U	D	1-1	Gemmill	40,608
34		13	(h)	Norwich C	W	3-1	Rioch, Gemmill, James	27,002
35		20	(a)	Middlesborough	W	2-0	Hector, George	24,120
36		24	(h)	Stoke C	D	1-1	Rioch (pen)	30,156
37		27	(h)	BirminghamC	W	4-2	Nish, Rioch, Davies, James	28,161
38	Apr	10	(a)	Manchester C	L	3-4	Rioch 2, Todd	42,061
39		17	(h)	Leicester C	D	2-2	Lee 2	30,085
40		19	(a)	Aston Villa	L	0-1		39,241
41		20	(h)	Everton	L	1-3	Rioch	22,488
42		24	(a)	Ipswich T	W	6-2	Lee 2, Hector 2, Rioch 2 (1 pen)	26,971

FINAL LEAGUE POSITION : 4th in Division One

Appearances

Sub. Appearances

Goals

Boulton	Thomas	Nish	Rioch	McFarland	Todd	Newton	Gemmill	Lee	Bourne	George	Hinton	Hector	Webster	Moseley	Davies	Powell	James	Daniel	Macken	King	
1	2	3	4	5	6	7	8	9	10*	11	12										1
1	2	3	4	5	6	7	8	9	10	11											2
1	2	3	4	5	6	7	8	9*		11	12	10									3
1	2	3	4	5	6	7	8	9		11		10									4
1	5	3	4		6	7	8	9*		11	12	10	2								5
1	5	3	4		6	7	8	9		11		10	2								6
	2	3	4	5	6	7	8	9		11		10		1							7
1	2	3	4	5	6	7	8	9		11		10									8
1	2	3	4	5	6	7	8	9*		11		10			12						9
1	2	3	4	5	6	7	8		9	11		10									10
1	2	3	4	5	6		8	9		11	12	10				7					11
1	2	3	4	5	6		8	9*		11		10			12	7					12
1	2	3	4	5	6	7	8	9		11*		10			12						13
1	2	3	4	5	6	7*	8	9		11		10			12						14
1	5	3	4*		6	7	8	9		11		10	2		12						15
1	2	3	4	5	6	7	8	9		11		10									16
1	2	3	4	5	6	7	8	9		11		10									17
1	5	3	4		6	7	8	9		11		10	2								18
1	2	3	4	5	6	7	8	9		11		10									19
1	2	3	4	5	6	7*	8	9		11		10			12						20
1	2	3	4	5	6	7	8	9		10							11				21
1	2	3	4	5	6	7	8			10*	12				9		11				22
1	2		4*	5	6	7	8			10	12				9		11	3			23
1	2				6	3	8			10					9	7	11	5	4		24
1	2		4	5	6	3	8			10		12			9	7*	11				25
	2	3	4	5	6		8	9		10				1		7	11				26
	2		4	5	6	3	8	9*		10				1	12	7	11				27
	2	3	4	5	6		8	9*		10				1	12	7	11				28
	2	3	4	5	6		8			10		9		1		7	11				29
	2	3	4	5	6		8			10		9		1		7	11				30
	2	3	4	5	6		8			10		9		1		7	11				31
	2	3		5	6	4	8			10		9		1	12	7*	11				32
	2	3		5	6	4	8	7		10		9		1	12		11*				33
		3	4	5	6		8					9	2	1	10	7	11				34
	2	3		5	6	4	8			10		9		1		7	11				35
	2	3	4	5	6		8			10*		9		1	12	7	11				36
	2	3	4	5*	6	12	8					9		1	10	7	11				37
	2*	3	4	5	6	12	8	9						1	10	7	11				38
	2	3	4*	5	6	12	8	9						1	10	7	11				39
	2		4	5	6	3	8	9						1	12	7	11		10*		40
	2*		4	5	6	3	8	9				10		1	12	7	11				41
			4	5*	6	3	8	9				10	2	1	12	7				11	42
24	40	35	38	37	42	30	42	28	4	35		29	6	18	8	20	21	2	2	1	
						3					3	3				13	1				
		2	13	2	1	1	5	12		16		9			3	3	6				

1976-77

1	Aug	21	(a)	Newcastle U	D	2-2	George, Nish	35,927
2		25	(h)	Middlesborough	D	0-0		23,344
3		28	(h)	Manchester U	D	0-0		30,054
4	Sep	4	(a)	Leeds U	L	0-2		33,352
5		11	(h)	Liverpool	L	2-3	George, Neal (og)	26,833
6		18	(a)	Norwich C	D	0-0		22,375
7		25	(h)	West Brom A	D	2-2	McFarland 2	24,378
8	Oct	2	(a)	Birmingham C	L	1-5	James	29,190
9		16	(h)	Tottenham H	W	8-2	Rioch 4, George 2 (1 pen), Todd, Thomas	24,219
10		23	(a)	Stoke C	L	0-1		20,916
11		30	(h)	Bristol C	W	2-0	George, Hector	22,252
12	Nov	6	(a)	Queen's Park R	D	1-1	Thomas	22,527
13		20	(a)	Everton	L	0-2		23,020
14		27	(h)	Sunderland	W	1-0	James	25,423
15	Dec	4	(a)	Manchester C	L	2-3	James 2	34,179
16		15	(h)	Arsenal	D	0-0		24,016
17		18	(a)	Ipswich T	D	0-0		23,234
18		27	(h)	Leicester C	W	1-0	James	32,892
19	Jan	15	(a)	Middlesborough	L	0-2		17,914
20		22	(h)	Newcastle U	W	4-2	Hales 2, McFarland, Powell	23,036
21	Feb	5	(a)	Manchester U	L	1-3	Macken	54,044
22		12	(h)	Leeds U	L	0-1		28,350
23		19	(a)	Liverpool	L	1-3	Hector	44,202
24	Mar	2	(a)	Aston Villa	L	0-4		37,396
25		5	(a)	West Brom A	L	0-1		19,280
26		9	(h)	Coventry C	D	1-1	Daniel	22,808
27		12	(h)	Birmingham C	D	0-0		25,256
28		15	(a)	Bristol C	D	2-2	Hales, Daly	18,552
29		23	(a)	Tottenham H	D	0-0		27,359
30	Apr	2	(h)	Stoke C	W	2-0	James, Daly (pen)	23,161
31		6	(h)	Norwich C	D	2-2	James, Powell	21,342
32		9	(h)	Aston Villa	W	2-1	Hales, James	28,061
33		12	(a)	Leicester C	D	1-1	Powell	22,393
34		16	(h)	Everton	L	2-3	Daly 2 (1 pen)	23,443
35		20	(h)	West Ham U	D	1-1	Daly (pen)	21,380
36		23	(a)	Sunderland	D	1-1	Powell	35,490
37		25	(a)	Coventry C	L	0-2		15,788
38		30	(h)	Manchester C	W	4-0	Daly (pen), Gemmill, Hector, Daniel	29,127
39	May	3	(a)	Arsenal	D	0-0		26,659
40		7	(a)	West Ham U	D	2-2	James, McGivern (og)	32,079
41		11	(h)	Queen's Park R	W	2-0	McFarland, Daly	21,312
42		14	(h)	Ipswich T	D	0-0		24,491

FINAL LEAGUE POSITION : 15th in Division One

Appearances

Sub. Appearances

Goals

Moseley	Thomas	Nish	Rioch	McFarland	Todd	Newton	Gemmill	George	Hector	James	Daniel	King	Bourne	Carruthers	Macken	Webster	Powell	Boulton	Hales	Langan	Daly	O'Riordan	
1	2	3	4	5	6	7	8	9	10	11													1
1	2	3	10	5	6	7	8			11	4	9											2
1	2	3	4	5	6	7	8	9		11			10*	12									3
1	2	3	9	5	6	7*	8	10		11		12			4								4
1	2	3	4	5	6	7	8	10	9	11													5
1	2	3	4	5	6	7	8	10	9	11													6
1		3	4	5	6	7*	8	10	9	11					12	2							7
1	2	3	4		6*	7	8	9		11	5	12			10								8
1	2	3	9	5	6		8	10		11					4	7							9
1	2	3	9	5	6			10		11	12	8			4*	7							10
1	2		9	5	6	3		10*	12	11		8			4	7							11
	2		9	5	6	3	8		10	11					4	7	1						12
	2		9		6	3	8		10*	11	5		12		4	7	1						13
	2			5	6	3	8		10	11		9			4	7	1						14
	2				6	3	8	10		11	5	9			4	7	1						15
	2			5	6	3	8		10	11					4	7	1		9				16
	2			5	6	3	8		10	11					4	7	1		9				17
	2			5	6		8		10	11	3				4	7	1		9				18
	2			5	6	3	8		10	11			12		4	7*	1		9				19
				5	6		8		10	11*	3		12		4	2	7	1	9				20
	2			5	6				10	11	3	8			4	7	1		9				21
					6	3			10	8	11	5	4	12			7*	1	9	2			22
					6	7			10	8	11*	5	4		12	3		1	9	2			23
					6	7			10	9	11	5	4		8	3		1		2			24
	3				6	7			10	9	11	5	4		8			1		2			25
	3			5*	6				10	7	11	12			8			1	9	2	4		26
					6				10	8	11	5				3	7	1	9	2	4		27
					6				10	8	11	5				3	7	1	9	2	4		28
					6	7			10*	9	11	5	8			3		1		2	4	12	29
				5		7	8		10	11						3	6	1	9	2	4		30
				5	6		8	10	9*	11						3	7	1	12	2	4		31
				5	6		8	10		11						3	7	1	9	2	4		32
				5	6		8	10		11						3	7	1	9	2	4		33
					6	12	8		10	11	5					3*	7	1	9	2	4		34
				5	6		8		10	11						3	7	1	9	2	4		35
				5	6	12	8		10	11						3	7	1	9	2	4*		36
1				5	6			10	9	11	7					3	8			2	4		37
				5	6	11	8		10		9					3	7	1		2	4		38
				5	6	11	8		10		3					2	7	1	9		4		39
				5	6		8	10	9	11						3	7	1		2	4		40
				5	6		8	10	9	11						3	7	1		2	4		41
				5	6		8	10	9		3	11					7	1		2	4		42
12	21	10	13	31	41	25	30	29	28	39	19	10	3		18	19	29	30	17	21	17		
					2				1		2	2	4	1	2			1			1		
	2	1	4	4	1		1	5	3	9	2				1		4			4		7	

31

1977-78

1	Aug	20	(a)	Coventry C	L	1-3	Nish	17,938
2		24	(h)	Ipswich T	D	0-0		19,809
3		27	(a)	Nottingham F	L	0-3		28,807
4	Sep	3	(h)	Manchester U	L	0-1		21,279
5		10	(a)	Chelsea	D	1-1	Daly (pen)	25,759
6		17	(h)	Leeds U	D	2-2	Hughes, Gemmill	24,274
7		24	(a)	Liverpool	L	0-1		46,462
8	Oct	1	(h)	Middlesborough	W	4-1	Daly (pen), Hector, Hughes, Powell	21,040
9		4	(a)	Wolves	W	2-1	Hughes 2	21,571
10		8	(a)	Newcastle U	W	2-1	McFarland, Hughes	26,578
11		15	(a)	West Brom A	D	1-1	George	28,397
12		22	(a)	Birmingham C	L	1-3	O'Riordan	23,108
13		29	(h)	Norwich C	D	2-2	Daly, Hughes	21,957
14	Nov	5	(h)	Everton	L	0-1		29,335
15		12	(a)	Bristol C	L	1-3	Rioch	20,196
16		19	(h)	West Ham U	W	2-1	Rioch, Nish	23,273
17		26	(a)	Arsenal	W	3-1	Powell, Ryan, Rioch	31,989
18	Dec	3	(h)	Manchester C	W	2-1	Hughes, Ryan	26,888
19		10	(a)	Leicester C	D	1-1	Hughes	21,199
20		17	(h)	Bristol C	W	1-0	Todd	21,802
21		26	(a)	Queen's Park R	D	0-0		18,917
22		27	(h)	Aston Villa	L	0-3		30,395
23		31	(a)	Ipswich T	W	2-1	George, Ryan	20,870
24	Jan	2	(h)	Coventry C	W	4-2	George 3 (2 pen), Daly	25,929
25		14	(h)	Nottingham F	D	0-0		33,384
26		21	(a)	Manchester U	L	0-4		57,115
27	Feb	25	(a)	Middlesborough	L	1-3	Daly	20,703
28	Mar	4	(h)	Newcastle U	D	1-1	George (pen)	19,708
29		8	(h)	Liverpool	W	4-2	Daly 2, George, Crawford	23,413
30		11	(h)	Chelsea	D	1-1	Daniel	21,504
31		18	(h)	Birmingham C	L	1-3	Curran	19,843
32		25	(a)	Aston Villa	D	0-0		32,793
33		27	(h)	Queen's Park R	W	2-0	Daly, George	20,155
34		29	(a)	Norwich C	D	0-0		15,523
35	Apr	1	(a)	Everton	L	1-2	George	38,213
36		8	(h)	Wolves	W	3-2	Daly, Ryan, Masson	20,836
37		12	(a)	Leeds U	L	0-2		16,531
38		15	(a)	West Ham U	L	0-3		25,424
39		18	(a)	West Brom A	L	0-1		20,961
40		22	(h)	Leicester C	W	4-1	George 2, Rioch, Buckley	18,829
41		29	(a)	Manchester C	D	1-1	Daly	39,175
42	May	9	(h)	Arsenal	W	3-0	Curran, Chesters, Hill	18,189

FINAL LEAGUE POSITION : 12th in Division One

Appearances

Sub. Appearances

Goals

Boulton	Langan	Nish	Daly	McFarland	Todd	O'Riordan	King	Hales	Hector	Hughes	Gemmill	Webster	Powell	Thomas	George	James	Hunt	Macken	Daniel	Middleton	Ryan	Masson	Rioch	Curran	Chesters	Bartlett	Buckley	Crawford	Corish	Hill	
1	2	3	4	5	6	7	8	9	10	11																					1
1	2	3*	4	5	6	7		9	10	11	8	12																			2
1	2	3	4	5*	6			9	10	11	8	12	7																		3
1	2	3*	4		6			9		12	8		7	5	10	11															4
1	2		4		6			9		7	8	12	3	5	10	11*															5
1	2	3	4	5*	6				9	8			7		10	11		12													6
1	2	3	4		6				8	9			7		10	11			5												7
	2	3	4	5	6				8	9					10	11				1	7										8
	2	3	4	5		12			8	9			7		10	11*				1	6										9
	2	3*	4	5		12			8	9			7		10				6	1	11										10
	2	3	4	5	6					9			7		10	11				1		8									11
	2	3	4	5*	6	12			8	9			7		10	11				1											12
	2	3	4		6				8	9			7						5	1	11	10									13
1	2	3	4						8	9			7						5		11	10	6								14
	2	3		5	6				8	9			7							1	11	10	4								15
	2	3		5	6					8					10					1	11	9	4	7							16
	2	3		5	6					8					10					1	11	9	4	7							17
	2	3		5	6					8					10					1	11	9	4	7							18
	2*	3	8		6					12			5		10					1	11	9	4	7							19
	2	3*	4	5	6				8	12					10					1	11	9		7							20
	2		4		6								5		10				3	1	11	9	8	7							21
	2		4		6								8				5		3	1	11	9		7	10						22
	2		4		6								8		10		5		3	1	11*	9		7	12						23
	2		4		6								8		10*		5		3	1		9		7	12	11					24
	2		8		6					12					10				5	1	11*	9	4	7			3				25
	2		8		6										10				5	1	11*	9	4	7	12		3				26
	2		8		6										10		5			1		9	4	7	11		3				27
	2		8	5						12					10				6	1		9	4*	7	11		3				28
	2		8	5									4		10				6	1		9		7			3	11			29
	2		8	5*									4		10				6	1		9		7	12		3	11			30
	2		8		6										10				5	1		9*	4	7			3	11	12		31
	2		8		6								4		10				5	1		9		7			3	11			32
	2		8	5	6					9					10					1	11		4	7			3				33
	2		8	5	6					9*					10				12	1	11		4	7			3				34
	2		8	5	6										10				9	1	11		4*	7	12		3				35
	2		8	5	6								4		10					1	11	9		7			3				36
	2		8	5	6								4		10					1	11	9		7*	12		3				37
	2	11	8	5	6								7*		10					1		9	4		12		3				38
	2		8	5	6*										10				12	1	11		4	7	9		3				39
	2		8	5	6										10					1	11*		4	7	9		3		12		40
	2		8	5	6										10					1	11		4	7	9		3				41
	2			5	6								8		10					1			4	7	9		3			11	42
8	42	21	37	26	32	2	1	5	11	17	5		32	2	34	7	5		17	34	24	23	20	26	6	3	18	3		1	
											3			2		3	3		1		2				2	6			1		
		2	10	1	1	1		1	8	1		2			11				1			4	1	4	2	1		1	1	1	

33

1978-79

1	Aug	19	(h)	Manchester C	D	1-1	George	26,480
2		22	(a)	Everton	L	1-2	Nish	40,125
3		26	(a)	Birmingham C	D	1-1	Daly	21,973
4	Sep	2	(h)	Coventry C	L	0-2		21,435
5		9	(a)	Bolton W	L	1-2	Daly	20,331
6		16	(h)	West Brom A	W	3-2	Daly, Powell, Duncan	23,772
7		23	(h)	Southampton	W	2-1	George, Carter	21,623
8		30	(a)	Norwich C	L	0-3		15,930
9	Oct	7	(h)	Chelsea	W	1-0	Harris (og)	20,251
10		14	(a)	Liverpool	L	0-5		47,475
11		21	(h)	Tottenham H	D	2-2	Buckley, Duncan	26,181
12		28	(a)	Leeds U	L	0-4		25,449
13	Nov	4	(h)	Wolves	W	4-1	Daly, Hill, Duncan, Caskey	20,658
14		11	(a)	Manchester C	W	2-1	Daly (pen), Duncan	37,376
15		18	(h)	Birmingham C	W	2-1	Buckley, Daly	24,720
16		21	(a)	Coventry C	L	2-4	Daly (pen), Caskey	21,776
17		25	(h)	Queen's Park R	W	2-1	Daniel, Caskey	19,702
18	Dec	2	(a)	Bristol C	L	0-1		18,096
19		9	(h)	Manchester U	L	1-3	Daly	23,180
20		16	(a)	Arsenal	L	0-2		26,943
21		23	(h)	Aston Villa	D	0-0		20,109
22		26	(a)	Nottingham F	D	1-1	Daly (pen)	34,256
23	Feb	3	(a)	Southampton	W	2-1	Powell, Duncan	21,109
24		10	(h)	Norwich C	D	1-1	Buckley	17,837
25		24	(h)	Liverpool	L	0-2		27,859
26		28	(h)	Ipswich T	L	0-1		15,935
27	Mar	3	(a)	Tottenham H	L	0-2		28,089
28		10	(h)	Leeds U	L	0-1		22,800
29		13	(a)	Middlesborough	L	1-3	Daly (pen)	16,286
30		21	(h)	Bolton W	W	3-0	McFarland 2, Daly	15,227
31		24	(h)	Everton	D	0-0		20,814
32		26	(a)	West Brom A	L	1-2	Crawford	19,801
33		31	(a)	Queen's Park R	D	2-2	Daly, Crawford	13,988
34	Apr	4	(a)	Chelsea	D	1-1	McFarland	12,479
35		7	(h)	Bristol C	L	0-1		17,090
36		11	(a)	Aston Villa	D	3-3	Greenwood, Powell, Gibson (og)	21,884
37		14	(h)	Nottingham F	L	1-2	Webb	30,156
38		16	(a)	Ipswich T	L	1-2	Crawford	19,919
39		21	(h)	Arsenal	W	2-0	Buckley, Daly	18,674
40		24	(a)	Wolves	L	0-4		19,036
41		28	(a)	Manchester U	D	0-0		42,546
42	May	5	(h)	Middlesborough	L	0-3		18,151

FINAL LEAGUE POSITION : 19th in Division One

Appearances

Sub. Appearances

Goals

Player appearance / squad-number chart.

Middleton	Langan	Buckley	Daly	McFarland	Todd	Powell	Nish	Ryan	George	Hill	Daniel	Chesters	Carter	McCaffery	Duncan	Rioch	Caskey	Moreland	Clark	Bartlett	Clayton	McKellar	Webb	Wicks	Greenwood	Spooner	Crawford	Emson	#
1	2	3	4	5	6	7	8	9	10	11																			1
1	2	3	4	5	6	7	8	9	10	11																			2
1	2	3	4	5		7*	8	9	10	11	6	12																	3
1	2	3	4	5	6	9	8*	11	10		12		7																4
1	2	3	4	5	6	9	8	11	10				7																5
1	2	3	4	5		8	12	11*					7	6	9	10													6
1	2	3	4			6			10				7	5	9*	8	11	12											7
1	2	3	4	5		7	11						6		8	9		10											8
1	2	3	4			8			10				7	5	12	9	6*	11											9
1	2	3	4			8	12	10*					7	5		9	6	11											10
1	2	3	4			8	12						7	5	9		6		10*	11									11
1	2	3	4			8				11	5		7		9		6		10										12
1	2	3	4	5		8				11			7		9			10	6										13
1	2	3	4	5		8				11			7		9			10	6										14
1	2	3	4			8				11	5		7				10	6	9										15
1	2	3	4			8	12			11	5		7				9*	6	10										16
1	2	3	4			8					5		7		9		10	6	11										17
1	2	3	4	5*		8					12		7		9		10	6	11										18
1	2	3	4	5						11			7		9		10	6	8										19
		3	4			8				11	5		7			10	9	6		2		1							20
	2	3	4	5		8				11			7				9	12	10			1		6*					21
	2	3	4	5		8				11			7*				9	12	10			1		6					22
	2	3		5		8							10*	4			9	12	7			1		6	11				23
	2	3		5		8							7		9	4		10				1		6	11				24
	2	3	4	5		8							7		10		9	6				1			11				25
	2	3	4	5		8							7		12	10	9*					1		6	11				26
	2	3	4	5		8							10		9							1		6	11	7			27
	2	3	4			8							10*		9				7			1	5	6	11		12		28
	2	3	4			8									9				7			1	6	5	11	10			29
1	2	3	4	5		8							7					10					6	9	11				30
1	2	3	4	5		8							7					10					6	9	11				31
1	2	3	4*	5		8							7					10				12	6	9	11				32
1	2	3	4	5		8			12				7*					10					6	9	11				33
1	2	3	4	5		8							7*		12			10					6	9	11				34
1	2	3	4*			8							7		12			10					5	6	9		11		35
1	2	3		5		8											4	10					6	9	11		7		36
	2	3				8							7					4				1	5	6	9		11	10	37
	2	3				8							7					4				1	5	6	9		11	10	38
	2	3	4			8												10				1	5	6	9		11	7	39
		3	4			8												10	2			1	5	6	9		11	7	40
	2	3	4	5		8											9	10	7			1		6	11				41
	2	3	4			8											9	8*	6	7	10	1	5		12			11	42
26	40	42	37	24	4	41	6	6	8	12	6		29	6	16	7	22	27	17	3	1	16	9	19	19	1	12	6	
									4		2	1	1		1		1	2	4					1		1	1		
		4	13	3		3	1		2	1	1		1		5		3						1		1		3		

1979-80

1	Aug	18	(a)	West Brom A	D	0-0		24,643
2		22	(h)	Wolves	L	0-1		21,787
3		25	(h)	Everton	L	0-1		17,820
4	Sep	1	(a)	Crystal P	L	0-4		25,382
5		8	(h)	Arsenal	W	3-2	McCaffery, Langan, Duncan	16,429
6		15	(a)	Manchester U	L	0-1		54,308
7		22	(h)	Middlesborough	W	1-0	Duncan	18,620
8		29	(a)	Southampton	L	0-4		22,583
9	Oct	6	(h)	Bolton W	W	4-0	Duncan 2, Emson 2	16,810
10		9	(a)	Wolves	D	0-0		30,131
11		13	(a)	Tottenham H	L	0-1		33,269
12		20	(h)	Aston Villa	L	1-3	Emson	20,162
13		27	(a)	Stoke C	L	2-3	Hill 2	18,535
14	Nov	3	(h)	West Brom A	W	2-1	Hill, Emery	21,408
15		10	(a)	Bristol C	W	2-0	Moreland, Duncan	16,943
16		17	(h)	Ipswich T	L	0-1		16,699
17		24	(h)	Nottingham F	W	4-1	Duncan 2, Daly, Emery	27,729
18	Dec	1	(a)	Brighton & HA	L	0-2		23,013
19		8	(h)	Norwich C	D	0-0		15,381
20		15	(a)	Manchester C	L	0-3		27,664
21		22	(h)	Liverpool	L	1-3	Davies (pen)	24,945
22		26	(h)	Coventry C	L	1-2	Clark	15,531
23		29	(a)	Everton	D	1-1	Davies	22,554
24	Jan	1	(a)	Leeds U	L	0-1		24,271
25		12	(h)	Crystal P	L	1-2	Osgood	16,872
26		19	(a)	Arsenal	L	0-2		22,091
27	Feb	2	(h)	Manchester U	L	1-3	B. Powell	27,783
28		9	(a)	Middlesborough	L	0-3		15,587
29		16	(h)	Southampton	D	2-2	Davies, B. Powell	16,535
30		23	(h)	Tottenham H	W	2-1	McCaffery, Biley	21,183
31	Mar	1	(a)	Aston Villa	L	0-1		28,956
32		8	(h)	Stoke C	D	2-2	Biley, Osgood	22,695
33		15	(a)	Bolton W	W	2-1	Swindlehurst, Biley	13,236
34		22	(h)	Bristol C	D	3-3	Biley 3 (1 pen)	17,020
35		29	(a)	Ipswich T	D	1-1	Swindlehurst	19,882
36	Apr	5	(a)	Leeds U	W	2-0	B. Powell, Emson	22,745
37		7	(a)	Coventry C	L	1-2	McCaffery	19,519
38		8	(a)	Liverpool	L	0-3		40,939
39		12	(h)	Brighton & HA	W	3-0	Biley 2 (1 pen), Osgood	17,257
40		19	(a)	Nottingham F	L	0-1		32,266
41		26	(h)	Manchester C	W	3-1	Swindlehurst, Biley (pen), Reid (og)	22,572
42	May	3	(a)	Norwich C	L	2-4	McCaffery, Swindlehurst	15,173

FINAL LEAGUE POSITION : 21st in Division One

Appearances

Sub. Appearances

Goals

36

Middleton	Langan	Buckley	Rioch	McFarland	Wicks	McCaffery	Moreland	Caskey	Greenwood	Hill	Daly	Crawford	Webb	Duncan	Powell S.	Carter	Davies	Emery	Osgood	Emson	Spooner	Powell B.	McKellar	Clark	Bartlett	Whymark	Biley	Cherry	Swindlehurst	Wilson	Richards	#
1	2	3	4	5	6	7	8	9*	10	11	12																					1
1	2	.3		5	6	7	8	9*	10	11	4	12																				2
1	2	3	7	5	6	8		9*	10	11	4	12																				3
1	2	3	7	5	8				10	11	4*	12	6	9																		4
1	2	3		5	8	7				11	10*		6	9	4	12																5
1	2	3		5	8	7				11	12		6	9*	4	10																6
1	2	3		5	6				12		4*			9	8	7	10	11														7
1	2	3		5*	6	11			12					9	8	7	10	4														8
1	2	3	4	5	8									9			10	7	6	11												9
1	2	3	4	5	8				12					9*			10	7	6	11												10
1	2	3	4	5	8			9	10									7	6	11*		12										11
1	2	3	4	5	8			9									10	7	6	11												12
1	2*	3	4	5					12	11				9			10	7	6			8										13
	2	3	4	5						11				9			10	7	6			8	1									14
	2	3	5							11				9			10	7	6			8	1	4								15
	2	3	5			4*				11				9			10	7	6			8	1	12								16
	2	3									4*		5	9			10	7	6	12		8	1	11								17
	2	3							12		4		5	9				7	6			8	1	11			10*					18
	2	3				11					4		5	9			10	7	6			8	1									19
	2	3				11					4		5	9			10*	7	6	12		8	1									20
	2	3				11					4		5	9			10	7	6			8	1				9					21
	2	3									4		5				10	12	6	11		8	1			7	9*					22
	2	3									4		5	9			10		6	11		8	1			7						23
	2	3							9		4		5*	12			10		6	11		8	1			7						24
		3				11					4		5				10	2	6	12		8	1			7*	9					25
		3									4		5		7		10	2	6	11		8	1				9					26
	2	3	5				12				4		5		7		10		6	11		8	1				9*					27
	2	3	5										7	8	6		10	4	12					11*			9	1				28
	2	3	5												6	4*	10	7		11		8		12			9	1				29
	2	3	5	4											6*		10	7	12	11		8					9	1				30
	2	3	5								4							7	6	11		8	1				9		10			31
	2	3	5				12				4							7*	6	11		8	1				9		10			32
	2	3	5								4							7*	6	11			1	8			9		10			33
	2	3	5				12				4							7*	6	11		8	1				9		10			34
	2	3	5				12				7							4	6	11*		8	1				9		10			35
	2	3	5				12				7*							4	6	11		8	1				9		10			36
	2	3	5	4														7	6	11		8*	1	12			9		10			37
	2	3	5	4														7	6	11*			1	8			9		10	12		38
	2	3	5	4														7	6	12			1	8			9		10*	11		39
	2	3	5	4														7	6	12			1	8			9		10	11*		40
	2	3	5	4							6							7		11				8			9	1	10			41
	2	3	5*	4							6							7						8			9	1	10	11	12	42
13	40	42	13	20	5	25	11	4	7	9	20	1	16	16	17	3	22	26	31	20		25	25	11	1	2	18	4	12	3		
													6	4		1	4		1	1		1	1	6	1	3		1		1		
	1								4	1			3	1		7	3	2	3	4		3		1			9	4				

37

1980-81

#	Month	Date		Opponent	Result	Score	Scorers	Attendance
1	Aug	16	(a)	Cambridge U	L	0-3		9,558
2		20	(h)	Chelsea	W	3-2	B. Powell (pen), Biley, Chivers (og)	20,353
3		23	(a)	Luton T	W	2-1	Swindlehurst, Osgood	11,025
4		30	(h)	Bolton W	W	1-0	Swindlehurst	17,378
5	Sep	6	(h)	Blackburn R	D	2-2	Biley 2	18,159
6		13	(a)	Grimsby T	W	1-0	Swindlehurst	13,220
7		20	(h)	Wrexham	L	0-1		16,823
8		27	(a)	Orient	L	0-1		5,490
9	Oct	4	(h)	Sheffield W	W	3-1	Biley, Emson, Grant (og)	18,554
10		7	(a)	Watford	D	1-1	Osgood	11,799
11		11	(a)	Swansea C	L	1-3	Osgood (pen)	13,300
12		18	(h)	Queen's Park R	W	3-3	Sheridan 2, Emson	16,021
13		25	(a)	Bristol C	W	2-2	Emson, Wilson	12,049
14	Nov	1	(h)	Shrewsbury T	W	1-1	Biley	15,784
15		8	(a)	Notts C	W	0-0		16,560
16		12	(a)	Chelsea	D	3-1	Clark, Wilson, Reid	19,449
17		15	(h)	Cambridge U	L	0-3		15,179
18		22	(a)	Bristol R	D	1-1	Emson	6,258
19		26	(h)	West Ham U	W	2-0	Clark, Biley	18,446
20		29	(h)	Cardiff C	D	1-1	Wilson	15,581
21	Dec	6	(a)	Preston NE	W	3-0	Biley, Swindlehurst, Hector	6,120
22		13	(h)	Watford	D	1-1	Hector	16,464
23		20	(a)	West Ham U	L	1-3	Swindlehurst (pen)	24,671
24		26	(h)	Oldham A	W	4-1	Biley 2, Swindlehurst 2	16,958
25		27	(a)	Newcastle U	W	2-0	McFarland, Boam (og)	20,886
26	Jan	10	(h)	Bristol C	W	2-1	Biley, Gillies (og)	14,915
27		24	(a)	Bolton W	L	1-3	Wilson	9,937
28		31	(h)	Luton T	D	2-2	Wilson, Hector	16,479
29	Feb	7	(h)	Grimsby T	W	2-1	Emery, Swindlehurst	19,691
30		14	(a)	Blackburn R	L	0-1		12,533
31		21	(h)	Orient	D	1-1	McFarland	15,709
32		28	(a)	Wrexham	D	2-2	Swindlehurst (pen), Sheridan	6,485
33	Mar	7	(a)	Sheffield W	D	0-0		28,518
34		21	(a)	Queen's Park R	L	1-3	B. Powell	8,905
35		28	(h)	Bristol C	W	1-0	Swindlehurst	14,798
36		31	(h)	Swansea C	L	0-1		16,210
37	Apr	4	(a)	Shrewsbury T	L	0-1		6,668
38		11	(h)	Notts C	D	2-2	Osgood (pen), Wilson	17,922
39		18	(h)	Newcastle U	W	2-0	McFarland, Wilson	13,846
40		20	(a)	Oldham A	W	2-0	Buckley, Clayton	6,194
41	May	2	(a)	Cardiff C	D	0-0		7,577
42		6	(h)	Preston NE	L	1-2	Swindlehurst	15,050

FINAL LEAGUE POSITION : 6th in Division Two

Appearances

Sub. Appearances

Goals

Jones	Emery	Buckley	Powell S.	McFarland	Ramage	Clark	Powell B.	Biley	Swindlehurst	Emson	Osgood	Richards	Wilson	Skivington	Hector	Sheridan	Reid	Clayton	Duncan	Gibson	Spooner	
1	2	3	4	5	6	7	8	9	10	11												1
1	2	3	4		6	7	8	9	10	11	5											2
1	2	3	4		6	7	8	9	10	11*	5	12										3
1	2	3	4		6	7	8	9	10*	11	5		12									4
1	2	3	4		6	7	8	9		11	5		10									5
1	2	3	4		6		8	9	10	11	5				7							6
1	2	3	4		6		8	9	10	11	5				7							7
1	2	3	4	5	12		8	9	10	11	6			7*								8
1	2	3	4	5		7	8	9	10	11	6											9
1	2	3	4	5	7*	12	8	9	10	11	6											10
1	2	3	4	5*		7	8		9	11	6			12	10							11
1	2	3	5				8			11	6		9	7	10	4						12
1	2	3	5			8		9		11	6		12	7*	10	4						13
1	2	3	5			7		9	10	11	6			8		4						14
1	2	3	5			7		9	8	11	6			10		4						15
1	2				5	6	7	9	8	11*		3			10	4	12					16
1			5	6	4	7*	9	8				3			10	2	12	11				17
1			5	6	4	7	9	8		11		3			10	2						18
1		2	5	6	4	7	9	8		11		3			10							19
1		2	5	6	4	7*	9	8		11	12	3			10							20
1		2	5	6	4		9	10		11		3			8	7						21
1		2	5*	6	4		9	10		11		3	12		8	7						22
1	2		7	6	4		9	10		11	5	3			8							23
1	2		7	5	6	4	9	10		11		3			8*	12						24
1	2		7	5	6	4	9	10		11		3			8							25
1	2	3	4	5	6		8	9	10	11						7						26
1	2	3	4	5		7		9		11	6		10		8							27
1	2	3	4	5		7		9		11	6		10		8							28
1	2	3	4	5		7		9	6*	11	12		10		8							29
1	2	3		5	6	7		9	4	11	12		10*		8							30
1	2	3		5*	6	7		9	10		12		11		8		4					31
1	2	3			6	12			10		5		9		8	4	7	11*				32
1	2*	3	5		6				10		12		9		8	4	7	11				33
1	2	3	6	5		7			10		12		9		8	4		11*				34
1	2	3	4	5		6			10	11			7		8			9				35
1	2	3	4	5*		6			10	11			7		8		12	9				36
1	2	3	4			6			10				9*		8	5	7	11	12			37
1	2	3	4			6			10	11	5				8		7	9				38
1		3	4	5		6				11	2		10		8		7	9				39
1		3	4			6				11	2		10		8	5	7	9				40
1	4								10	11	2	3	9*		8	5	7	12		6		41
1		3		5					10	11	2		9*		8	4	7	12		6		42
42	32	32	36	23	23	20	29	29	34	36	26	8	24	9	25	10	12	7	3		2	
				1	2				2	4	1	3	1		1	3	2		1			
	1	1		3		2	2	10	11	4	4		7		3	3	1	1				

39

1981-82

1	Aug	29	(h)	Orient	L	1-2	Hector	12,424
2	Sep	1	(a)	Cambridge U	W	2-1	Swindlehurst, Emery	5,071
3		5	(a)	Shrewsbury T	L	1-4	Swindlehurst	4,373
4		12	(h)	Leicester C	W	3-1	Ramage, Hector, Buckley	16,046
5		19	(a)	Sheffield W	D	1-1	Powell S	24,002
6		23	(h)	Bolton W	L	0-2		11,966
7		26	(h)	QPR	W	3-1	Hector 2, Ramage	11,246
8	Oct	3	(a)	Charlton Ath	L	1-2	Emson	6,686
9		10	(a)	Newcastle U	L	0-3		17,224
10		17	(h)	Blackburn R	D	1-1	Powell B	10,572
11		24	(a)	Crystal Palace	W	1-0	Swindlehurst	11,292
12		31	(h)	Grimsby T	D	1-1	Clayton	11,706
13	Nov	7	(a)	Luton T	L	2-3	Osgood, Clayton	10,784
14		14	(h)	Wrexham	W	2-1	Buckley, Edwards (og)	10,956
15		21	(a)	Norwich C	L	1-4	Osgood	13,175
16		25	(h)	Cambridge U	W	2-1	Swindlehurst, Clayton	8,470
17		28	(h)	Chelsea	D	1-1	Osgood	13,963
18	Dec	4	(a)	Cardiff C	L	0-1		5,506
19	Jan	16	(a)	Orient	L	2-3	Hill, Fisher (og)	4,598
20		23	(h)	Oldham Ath	W	1-0	Swindlehurst	10,171
21		26	(a)	Watford	L	1-6	Emson	12,684
22		30	(h)	Sheffield W	W	3-1	Wilson 2, Sheridan	11,215
23	Feb	2	(a)	Rotherham U	L	1-2	Hill	7,487
24		6	(a)	Leicester C	L	1-2	Emson	14,132
25		13	(h)	Charlton Ath	D	1-1	Sheridan	10,846
26		20	(a)	QPR	L	0-3		8,890
27		27	(h)	Newcastle U	D	2-2	Wilson, Emson	12,257
28	Mar	6	(a)	Blackburn R	L	1-4	Swindlehurst	8,364
29		10	(h)	Shrewsbury T	D	1-1	Wilson	7,518
30		13	(h)	Crystal Palace	W	4-1	Wilson 2, Buckley, Skivington	10,248
31		20	(a)	Grimsby T	L	0-1		7,537
32		27	(h)	Luton T	D	0-0		15,836
33	Apr	3	(a)	Wrexham	D	1-1	Emson	4,073
34		10	(a)	Barnsley	D	0-0		13,457
35		12	(h)	Rotherham U	W	3-1	Wilson, Buckley, Skivington	14,080
36		17	(h)	Norwich C	L	0-2		12,508
37		24	(a)	Chelsea	W	2-0	Powell B, George	11,005
38		28	(h)	Barnsley	L	0-1		11,296
39	May	1	(h)	Cardiff C	D	0-0		10,111
40		4	(a)	Bolton W	L	2-3	Attley, George	5,226
41		8	(a)	Oldham Ath	D	1-1	Wilson	4,396
42		15	(h)	Watford	W	3-2	Hector, Wilson, Buckley	14,946

FINAL LEAGUE POSITION : 16th in Division Two

Appearances

Sub. Appearances

Goals

Jones	Coop	Richards	Powell S	Ramage	Hector	Spooner	Reid	Wilson	Swindlehurst	Emson	Emery	Buckley	Powell B	Cherry	Osgood	Gamble	Sheridan	Skivington	Clayton	Gibson	Money	Dalziel	Hill	Banovic	Attley	Lovatt	McAlle	George	Barton	
1	2	3	4	5	6	7	8	9*	10	11	12																			1
1	2	3	4	5	9	6	8		10			7	11																	2
1	2	3	4	5	9	6*	8		10	12		7	11																	3
1	2		4	5	9		8		10	11		7	3	6																4
1	2		4	5	9*		8	12	10	11		7	3	6																5
	2		4	5	9		8	12	10	11*		7	3	6	1															6
	2		4	5	9		8		10	11				6	1	3	7*	12												7
	2		4	5		7	8	9	10*	11		3		6	1		12													8
	2		4	5*	9				10	11		3	8		1		6	7	12											9
1	2		4				8		10	11		7	3	6			5		9											10
1	2		4				8		10	11		7	3	6			5		9											11
1	2		4			7	8		10	11*			3	6			5		9	12										12
1	2		4			8*		10		11			3	6			12	5	9											13
1	2		4			8			10	11		7	3	6			12	5	9*											14
1	2	4*			8				10	11		7	3	6			12	5	9											15
1	12	3			8				10	11	7*		4	6			2	5	9											16
1	7	3*			8				10	11			4	6			2	5	12	9										17
1	7	3			8*			9	10	11			4	6			2	5	12											18
1		3			7				10	11	2	4	8								5	6	9							19
1		3			7				10	11	2	3	8				5				6	4	9							20
1	11*				7				10	12	2	3	8				5				6	4	9							21
					7			10		11	2	3	8				5	12			6	4*	9	1						22
	12				7			10		11	2*	3	8				5	4			6		9	1						23
		4*			7			8	10	11		3					5	6	9					1	2	12				24
					7				10	11		3	8				5	4	9					1	2		6			25
					7				10	11		3	8				5	4	9					1	2		6			26
									10	11		3	8				5	4	9					1	7	2	6			27
					4				10	11		3	8				5		9					1	7	2	6			28
					7			9	10	11		3	8				5	4						1	2*	12	6			29
					7			9	10	11		3	8				5	4						1	2		6			30
					12			9	10	11		3	8				5	4						1	2*		6	7		31
								9	10	11		3					5	4						1	8		6	7	2	32
								9	10	11		3					5	4						1	8		6	7	2	33
					12			9*	10	11		3					5	4						1	8		6	7	2	34
								9	10	11		3					5	4						1	8		6	7	2	35
					12			9*	10	11		3					5	4						1	8		6	7	2	36
									10	11		3	7				5	4						1	8		6	9	2	37
					12				10	11		3	7				5	4*						1	8		6	9	2	38
									10	11		3	7				5	4						1	8		6	9	2	39
					12				10	11		3	7				5	4						1	8		6	9	2*	40
					12			9	10	11		3	8				5	4						1	2		6	7*		41
					7			8	10	11		3					5						9	1	4		6		2	42
17	17	8	16	9	27	4	12	20	36	39	15	40	32	4	4	1	31	21	13		5	4	6	21	19	2	18	11	10	
	1	1		4				4			2	1			3	1	1	3	1	1					2					
		1	2	5				9	6	5	1	5	2		3		2	2	3				2		1		2			

41

1982-83

1	Aug	28	(h)	Carlisle U	L	0-3		11,207
2	Sep	4	(a)	QPR	L	1-4	Gamble	10,217
3		8	(h)	Chelsea	W	1-0	Buckley (pen)	8,075
4		11	(h)	Middlesbrough	D	1-1	Dalziel (pen)	9,050
5		18	(a)	Leeds U	L	1-2	Brolly	17,052
6		25	(h)	Blackburn R	l	1-2	Dalziel	9,361
7	Oct	2	(a)	Chalton A	D	1-1	Gamble	4,685
8		9	(h)	Cambridge U	D	1-1	Brolly	8,135
9		16	(a)	Grimsby T	D	1-1	Swindhurst	7,684
10		19	(a)	Barnsley	D	1-1	Brolly	10,343
11		23	(h)	Leicester C	L	0-4		13,191
12		30	(a)	Wolves	l	1-2	Wilson	13,804
13	Nov	6	(a)	Sheffield W	l	0-2		17,924
14		13	(h)	Bolton W	D	0-0		10,999
15		20	(h)	Oldam A	D	2-2	Swindhurst	11,775
16		27	(a)	Burnley	D	1-1	Richards	7,513
17	Dec	4	(h)	Rotherham U	W	3-0	Swindhurst2, Dalziel	13,149
18		11	(a)	Fulham	L	1-2	Buckley	7,854
19		18	(h)	Crystal Palace	D	1-1	Richards	13,207
20		27	(a)	Newcastle U	L	0-1		30,558
21		29	(h)	Shewsbury T	L	2-3	Davison 2	13,068
22	Jan	1	(a)	Oldam A	D	2-2	Swindhurst, Gemmill (pen)	7,085
23		3	(h)	QPR	W	2-0	Swindhurst, Mills	14,007
24		15	(a)	Carlisle U	L	0-3		47,321
25		22	(h)	Leeds U	D	3-3	Swindhurst, Davison, Gemmill (pen)	17,005
26	Feb	5	(a)	Chelsea	W	3-1	Mills, Gemmill (pen), Bumstead (og)	8,661
27		26	(h)	Grimsby T	W	2-0	Davison, Moore K (og)	12,775
28	Mar	5	(a)	Leicester C	D	1-1	Barton	15,452
29		12	(h)	Wolves	D	1-1	Swindhurst	17,644
30		15	(a)	Cambridge U	D	0-0		4,476
31		19	(h)	Sheffield W	D	0-0		16,925
32		26	(a)	Bolton W	W	2-0	Brolly, Wilson	7,041
33	Apr	2	(a)	Shewsbury T	D	1-1	Hooks	7,194
34		5	(h)	Newcastle U	W	2-1	Hooks, Wilson	19,779
35		9	(a)	Middlebrough	W	3-2	Davison 2, Gemmill (pen)	9,078
36		13	(h)	Charlton A	D	1-1	Gemmill	15,605
37		16	(h)	Barnsley	D	1-1	Burns	14,861
38		23	(a)	Rotherham U	D	1-1	Gemmill (pen)	9,646
39		30	(h)	Burnley	W	2-0	Wilson, Davison	14,671
40	May	2	(a)	Blackburn	L	0-2		5,619
41		7	(a)	Crystal Palace	L	1-4	Gilbert (og)	8,464
42		14	(h)	Fulham	W	1-0	Davison	21,124

FINAL LEAGUE POSITION : 13th in Division Two

Appearances

Sub. Appearances

Goals

42

Banovic V	Barton J	Attley B	Powell S	Foster G	McAlle J	Brooly M	Skivington G	Wilson K	Swindhurst D	Reid A	Emson	Gamble F	Hill A	Buckley S	Dalziel I	Blades P	Mills G	Cherry S	Gemmill A	Richards J	Davison R	Fucher P	Thomas A	Hooks P	Burns K	
1	2	3	4	5	6	7	8*	9	10	11	12															1
1	2	3	4*	5	6	7	8		10	11		9	12													2
1	2*	8		5	6	7	4		10			12	9	3	11											3
1	2			5	6	7	4		10	8	11		9		3											4
1	2	8	5*			7	4		10			12	9	3	11	6										5
1	2	4	5	6	7	8			10*			9	12	3	11											6
1	2	4	6	5	7				10		12	8*	9	3	11											7
1	2	4	6	5	7				10		12	8*	9	3	11											8
1	2	4	5	6	7			9	10		11			3			8									9
1	2	4	5	6	7			9	10		11			3			8									10
1	2	4	5	6	7			9	10		11			3			8									11
	2	4	5	6	7	8	9		10					3	11			1								12
	2	4	5		7	6	9		10					3	11		8	1								13
	2	4*	5	6	7	12	8		10				9	3	11			1								14
	2	4	5	6	7				10					3	11			1	8	9						15
	2	4	5		7				10					3	11	6		1	8	9						16
	2	4	5		7				10					3	11	6		1	8	9*	12					17
	2	4	5		7				10					3	11	6		1	8	9*	12					18
	2	4*	5		7				10					3	11	6		1	8	9	12					19
	2*	3	5		4	12			10						11	6		1	8	9	7					20
	12	3	5	6	7				10						11*		2	1	4	9	8					21
	2	3	5	6	7				10						11			1	4	9	8					22
	2	3	5	6	7				10						11			1	4	9	8					23
	2	3	5		4	7	12		10						11	6*		1		9	8					24
	2		5	6	7	12	9		10					3	11			1	4*		8					25
	2	3	5		7		9		10						11			1	4		8	6				26
	2		5		7		9		10					3	11			1	4		8	6				27
	2		5		7				10				9	3	11			1	4		8	6				28
	2		5		7				10				9	3	11			1	4		8	6				29
	2		5		7				10				9	3	11			1	4		8	6				30
	2	4	5		7				10		11			3				1	8	9*	6	12				31
	2		5		7		9								3			1	4		8	6		10		32
	2		5		7		9								3			1	4		8	6		10		33
	2		5*		7		9								3			1	4		8	6		10	12	34
	2		5		7	12	9								3			1	4		8	6		10*	11	35
	2		5		7	12	9				11				3*			1	4		8	6		10		36
	2		5		7		9				11							1	4		8	6		10	3	37
	2		5		7	12	9				11*							1	4		8	6		10	3	38
	2		5*		7	12	9				11							1	4		8	6		10	3	39
	2	3	5	4	7		9		10						11			1			8	6				40
	2	3	5	4	7		9	10			12				11*			1			8	6				41
	2		5		7	12	9				11							1	4*		8	6		10	3	42
11	39	22	23	30	19	41	9	22	28	3	11	4	12	26	18	6	18	31	25	10	23	17		8	6	
1				5	1	3					5		3								3		1		1	
1					4			4	8			2		2	4		2		6	2	8			2	1	

43

1983-84

1	Aug	27	(a)	Chelsea	L	0-5		17,338
2		29	(h)	Sheffeild W	D	1-1	Davison	10,240
3	Sep	3	(h)	Swansea C	W	2-1	Davison, Campbell	9,711
4		4	(a)	Brighton & HA	L	0-1		10,886
5		10	(a)	Blackburn R	L	1-5	Campbell	5,837
6		17	(h)	Oldam A	D	2-2	Campbell 2	11,775
7		24	(a)	Charlton	L	0-1		5,638
8	Oct	1	(h)	Carlisle	L	1-4	Davison	12,041
9		8	(h)	Barnsley	L	0-2		12,611
10		15	(a)	Crystal Palace	W	1-0	Roberson	7,081
11		22	(a)	Huddersfield T	L	0-3		10,752
12		29	(h)	Grimsby T	L	1-2	Davison	11,688
13	Nov	5	(a)	Cambridge U	W	1-0	Davison	3,638
14		12	(h)	Middlesbrough	W	1-0	Davison	12,683
15		19	(h)	Leeds U	D	1-1	Davison	16,974
16		26	(a)	Manchester C	D	1-1	Plummer	22,689
17	Dec	3	(h)	Newcastle U	W	3-2	Davison, Gemmill (pen)	18,691
18		10	(a)	Portsmouth	L	0-3		11,834
19		17	(h)	Shewsbury T	W	1-0	Plummer	11,265
20		26	(a)	Fulham	D	2-2	Wilson 2	7,480
21		27	(h)	Cardiff C	L	2-3	McAlle, Hooks	16,054
22		31	(a)	Swansea C	L	0-2		6,578
23	Jan	2	(h)	Charlton A	L	0-1		12,808
24		14	(h)	Chelsea	L	1-2	Plummer	16,727
25		21	(a)	Oldam A	L	0-3		4,564
26	Feb	4	(a)	Carlisle U	L	1-2	Powell	4,417
27		11	(h)	Blackburn R	D	1-1	Gemmill (pen)	13,020
28		21	(a)	Grimsby T	L	1-2	Garner	8,545
29		25	(h)	Huddersfield T	D	1-1	Roberson (pen)	13,525
30	Mar	3	(h)	Cambridge U	W	1-0	Davison	12,007
31		17	(h)	Brighton & HA	L	0-3		10,560
32		20	(a)	Middlesbrough	D	0-0		5,735
33		31	(a)	Bansley	L	1-5	Davison	6,500
34	Apr	7	(h)	Crystal Palace	W	3-0	Garner 3	10,903
35		10	(a)	Sheffield W	L	1-3	Davison	22,041
36		14	(a)	Leeds U	D	0-0		12,542
37		21	(h)	Fulham	W	1-0	Garner	12,087
38		23	(a)	Cardiff C	L	0-1		5,156
39		28	(h)	Manchester C	W	1-0	Watson	14,470
40	May	5	(a)	Newcastle U	L	0-4		35,866
41		9	(h)	Portsmouth	W	2-0	Davison 2	10,189
42		12	(a)	Shewsbury T	L	2-3		5,562

FINAL LEAGUE POSITION : 20th in Division Two

Appearances

Sub. Appearances

Goals

Cherry S	Barton J	Buckley S	Gemmill A	Powell S	Fucher P	Plummer C	Davison R	Campell R	Hooks P	Roberson J	Attley B	McAlle J	O'Brein R	McFarland R	Hill A	Pratley R	Harbey G	Watson D	Wilson K	Blades P	Deacy E	Lane S	Findlay J	Garner A	Burns K	Banovic V	Devine S	#
1	2	3*	4	5	6	7	8	9	10	11	12																	1
1	2		4	5*	6	7	8	9	10	11	3	12																2
1	2		4		6	7	8	9	10	11			3	5														3
1	2		4		6	7		9	10	11		12	3	5*	8													4
1	2		4		6	8		9	10	11	2	5	3															5
1	2		4		6	7	8	9	10	11		3				5												6
1	2		4	7	6		8*	9	10	11				12			3	5										7
1	2*		4	7	6	12	8	9	10	11							3	5										8
1			4	10	6	7	8			11				6			3	5	9	2								9
1			4	2	6	7	8	9		11							3	5	10									10
1			4	2	6	7	8	9		11							3	5	10									11
1			4		6	7	8	9	10	11							3	5	12		2*							12
1		3	4	6			8		10	11	7							5	9		2							13
1		3	4	6			8		11*		7			12				5	9		2							14
1		3	4		6		8				7			12				5	9		2		11*					15
1		3	4	6		10	8					7		12			11*	5	9		2							16
1		3	4	6		10	8				2	7					11	5	9									17
1		3	4	6		10	8				2	7		12			11*	5	9									18
1		3	4	6		10	8			11	2	7						5	9									19
1		3	4	6		10	8			11	2	7						5	9									20
1		3	4	6		10	8			11	2	7						5	9									21
1		3	4	6		10	8			11	2	7						5	9									22
	2	3	4	6		10	8			11		7						5	9			1						23
1	2	3	4	6		10	8			11		7						5	9									24
1	2	3	4	6	7	10	8			11								5	9									25
1	2	3	4	6	7	12	8			11							10*	5	9									26
1	2	3	4	6	7		8	10	11									5	9									27
1	2	3	4	6*	7	12	8			11								5	9					10				28
1	2	3	4		7		8			11		6							9					10	5			29
1	2	3	4	6	7	12	8			11									9					10*	5			30
	2	3		4		7	8				11							5	9					10	6	1		31
	2	3		4			8			11	7	10						5	9						6	1		32
	2	3		4			8			11	7	10*						5	9						6	1	12	33
1		3	4	6			8			11							10*	5	12					9	2		7	34
1		3	4	6			8			11							10	5	12					9	2		7	35
1		3	4	6			8			11							10	5	12	2				9			7	36
1		3	4	6			8			11							10	5	12	2				9*			7	37
1		3	4	6			8			11						12	10	5		2*				9			7	38
1		3	4	6			8			11							10	5	12					9*	2		7	39
1		3	4	6			8			11							10	5	12					9*	2		7	40
1		3	4	6			8			11							10	5	12					9	2		7*	41
1		3	4	6			8			11							10	5	12					9*			7	42
38	19	31	38	36	18	23	40	11	17	31	13	14	4	3	1	1	19	34	24	4	5	1	1	13	11	3	9	
				4								5	1	2					8								1	
		2	1			3	14	4	1	2	1						1	2						5				

1984-85

1	Aug	25	(a)	Bournemouth	L	0-1			7,794
2	Sep	1	(h)	Bolton W	W	3-2	Wilson 3		11,488
3		8	(a)	Preston NE	L	1-2	Wilson		5,425
4		15	(h)	Burnley	D	2-2	Davison, Taylor		11,755
5		19	(h)	Bristol C	W	1-0	Wilson		11,314
6		22	(a)	Reading	D	0-0			5,423
7		29	(h)	Lincoln C	W	2-0	Burns, Wilson		12,244
8	Oct	2	(a)	Millwall	L	1-2	Wilson		5,923
9		6	(a)	Bristol R	L	1-2	Davison		7,862
10		13	(h)	Plymouth A	W	3-1	Buckley (pen), Davison 2		11,316
11		20	(h)	Hull C	W	3-1	Biggins, Davison, Taylor		13,422
12		23	(a)	Walsall	D	0-0			9,733
13		27	(a)	Rotherham U	L	0-2			8,508
14	Nov	7	(h)	Brentford	W	1-0	Davison		10,530
15		10	(a)	Bradford C	L	1-3	Palmer		8,650
16		24	(h)	Wigan A	D	2-2	Davison 2		10,364
17		28	(h)	Doncaster R	W	3-1	Davison 3		10,901
18	Dec	1	(a)	Cambridge U	W	2-0	Davison, Powell		3,424
19		15	(h)	Orient	W	1-0	Garner		10,328
20		22	(h)	Newport Co	D	3-3	Davison, Garner, Robertson		11,437
21		26	(a)	Gillingham	L	2-3	Buckley, Davison		7,140
22		29	(a)	Swansea C	W	5-1	Buckley, Davison, Garner, Wilson, Palmer		5,187
23	Jan	1	(h)	York C	W	1-0	Davison		16,113
24		12	(a)	Bolton W	L	0-3			6,491
25		30	(h)	Bournemouth	L	2-3	Buckley (pen), Pratley		9,181
26	Feb	2	(a)	Lincoln C	D	0-0			5,892
27		22	(a)	Doncaster R	L	1-2	Davison		5,713
28		26	(a)	Bristol C	L	0-3			8,729
29	Mar	2	(h)	Rotherham U	D	1-1	Christie		10,259
30		6	(h)	Walsall	W	2-0	Christie, Hooks		9,157
31		9	(a)	Hull C	L	2-3	Buckley, Christie		9,782
32		13	(h)	Preston NE	W	2-0	Buckley (pen), Hindmarch		8,248
33		16	(a)	Plymouth A	W	1-0	Davison		6,117
34		23	(h)	Bristol R	D	0-0			10,041
35		30	(a)	Brentford	D	1-1	Micklewhite		4,423
36	Apr	3	(h)	Millwall	L	1-2	Micklewhite		10,394
37		6	(h)	Gillingham	W	1-0	Davison		10,002
38		8	(a)	York C	D	1-1	Davison		6,797
39		13	(h)	Bradford C	D	0-0			14,063
40		17	(h)	Reading	W	4-1	Buckley, Christie, Davison, Micklewhite		7,945
41		20	(a)	Wigan A	L	0-2			4,015
42		23	(a)	Burnley	W	1-0	Christie		3,484
43		27	(h)	Cambridge U	W	1-0	Davison		8,539
44	May	4	(a)	Orient	D	2-2	Davison, Micklewhite		3,032
45		6	(h)	Swansea C	D	1-1	Christie		10,117
46		11	(a)	Newport Co	W	3-1	Christie (pen), Davison, Harbey		4,003

FINAL LEAGUE POSITION : 7th in Division Three

Appearances

Sub. Appearances

Goals

46

Steele	Palmer	Buckley	Richardson	Powell	Burns	Taylor	Wilson	Davison	Hooks	Robertsen	Hindmarch	Burridge	Streete	Biggins	Pratley	Lewis	Garner	Blades	Ablett	Christie	Micklewhite	Sutton	Devine	Williams	Harbey	
1	2	3	4	5	6	7	8	9	10	11																1
1	2	3	12	4	6	7	8	9	10*	11	5															2
1	2	3	12	4	6*	7	8	9	10	11	5															3
1	2	3	12	4	6	7	8	9	10	11*	5															4
1	2	3		4	6	7	8	9	10	11	5															5
	2	3		4	6	7	8	9	10	11		1	5													6
	2	3	12	4*	6	7	8	9	10	11		1	5													7
	2	3	4		6	7	8	9	10	11		1	5													8
	2	3	12	4	6	7	8	9	10*	11		1	5													9
	2	3		4	6	7	8	9	10	11		1	5													10
	2	3		4	6	7		9	10	11		1	5	8												11
1	2	3		4	6	7		9	10	11	5			8												12
1	2	3	12	4	6	7		9	10*	11	5			8												13
1	2	3		4	6	7		9	10	11	8		5													14
1	2	3	7	4	6			9	10	11	8		5													15
1	2	3		4		7		9	10*	11	5			8	12	6										16
1	2	3		4		7		9		11	5					6	10	8								17
1	2	3		4		7		9		11	5					6	10	8								18
1	2	3		4	6	7		9		11	5						10	8								19
1	2	3	12	4*	6	7		9		11	5						10	8								20
1	2	3	7		6		11	9			5				4		10	8								21
1	2	3	4			7	8	9*			5				12	6	10	11								22
1	2	3	4			7	8	9			5					6	10	11								23
1		3	4	12	7*			9			5			8	6	10	11	2								24
1		3		4	2			9		11*	5				12	6	10	8		7						25
1	2	3		4				9		11	5					6	10	8*	12	7						26
1		3						9	12	11	6	7	5	4		2	8*		10							27
1		3	4*					9	12	11	6		5	10		2		8	7							28
		3						9	10	11	5	6				4	2		8	7	1					29
	2	3						9	10	11	5					4	6		8	7	1					30
	2	3						9	10	11*	5					4	6	12	8	7	1					31
	2	3						9	10*	11	5					4	6	12	8	7	1					32
	2	3	12					9		11*	5					4	6		8	7	1	10				33
		3	4					9	10*	11	5	2					6	12	8	7	1					34
		3						9		11	5	2				4	6		8	7	1			10		35
		3						9		11	5	2				4*	6		8	7	1			10	12	36
		3	4					9		11	5	2					12	6	8*	7	1			10		37
		3	4					9			5	2						6	8	7	1			10	11	38
		3	4					9		11	5	2						6	8	7	1			10		39
		3	4*					9		11	5	2					12	6	8	7	1			10		40
		3						9		11	5	2					4	6	8	7	1			10		41
	2	3						9		11	5						4*	6	8	7	1			10	12	42
1	2	3						9		11	5						4	6	8	7				10		43
1	2	3						9		11	5					4		6	8	7				10		44
1	2	3						9		11*	5					4	12	6	8	7				10		45
1	2	3						9		11	5							6	8	7				10	4	46
26	33	46	7	27	19	22	13	46	21	41	22	6	30	8	12	22	13	21	3	20	19	14	1	12	2	
			7	1	1				2					2	1		3	1	3					2		
	2	7		1	1	2	8	24	1	1	1			1	1		3			7	4			1		

47

1985-86

1	Aug	17	(h)	Bournemouth	W	3-0	Christie, Chandler 2	11,324
2		24	(a)	Wigan A	L	1-2	Chandler	4,707
3		26	(h)	Wolverhampton W	W	4-2	Lewis, Christie 2, Davison	13,154
4		31	(a)	Bristol R	D	0-0		4,961
5	Sep	7	(h)	Blackpool	L	1-2	Davison	10,702
6		14	(a)	Bury	D	1-1	Hindmarch	3,684
7		17	(a)	Bristol C	D	1-1	Davison	7,750
8		21	(h)	Chesterfield	D	0-0		13,259
9		28	(a)	Cardiff C	W	2-0	MacLaren (pen), Christie	3,435
10	Oct	2	(h)	Swansea C	W	5-1	Christie, Davison 2, Chandler, Micklewhite	9,169
11		5	(h)	Notts Co	W	2-0	Chandler (pen), Davison	14,406
12		19	(h)	York C	W	2-1	Garner 2	11,157
13		22	(a)	Gillingham	W	2-1	Garner, Chandler	4,613
14		26	(h)	Plymouth A	L	1-2	Davison	11,433
15	Nov	2	(a)	Rotherham U	D	1-1	Williams	6,030
16		6	(a)	Brentford	D	3-3	Hindmarch 2, Davison	4,707
17		9	(h)	Lincoln C	W	7-0	Chandler, Davison, Micklewhite 2, Hindmarch 2, Garner	10,560
18		23	(a)	Bolton W	W	1-0	Micklewhite	5,887
19		30	(h)	Reading	D	1-1	Davison	16,140
20	Dec	15	(a)	Doncaster R	W	3-0	Davison 2, Micklewhite	4,617
21		22	(h)	Wigan A	W	1-0	Christie	14,047
22		28	(a)	Wolverhampton W	W	4-0	Williams, Christie, Davison, Gregory	9,166
23	Jan	18	(a)	Bournemouth	D	1-1	Micklewhite	4,223
24	Feb	1	(a)	Blackpool	W	1-0	Garner	6,732
25		8	(a)	York C	W	3-1	Micklewhite 2, Christie	5,994
26		22	(a)	Chesterfield	L	0-1		9,394
27	Mar	1	(h)	Cardiff C	W	2-1	Gregory, MacLaren	11,014
28		8	(a)	Notts Co	W	3-0	Micklewhite, Davison 2	13,086
29		12	(a)	Walsall	W	3-1	Chandler, Williams, Hart (og)	13,434
30		15	(h)	Darlington	D	1-1	Christie	11,824
31		19	(h)	Bristol C	W	2-0	Gregory, Christie	11,113
32		22	(a)	Plymouth A	L	1-4	Christie	11,769
33		29	(h)	Newport Co	D	1-1	Gregory	11,251
34		31	(a)	Walsall	D	1-1	MacLaren	8,294
35	Apr	5	(h)	Brentford	D	1-1	Micklewhite	11,026
36		7	(h)	Gillingham	W	2-0	Davison, Micklewhite	11,351
37		9	(h)	Bristol R	L	0-2		11,033
38		12	(a)	Lincoln C	W	1-0	Davison	6,237
39		19	(h)	Bolton W	W	2-1	Buckley, Williams	12,232
40		22	(a)	Newport Co	D	1-1	Christie	3,049
41		26	(a)	Reading	L	0-1		12,266
42		30	(h)	Bury	D	1-1	MacLaren (pen)	11,790
43	May	3	(h)	Doncaster R	D	1-1	Hindmarch	12,030
44		6	(a)	Swansea C	W	3-0	Christie 2 (1 pen), Chandler	3,974
45		9	(h)	Rotherham U	W	2-1	Gee, Christie (pen)	21,036
46		12	(a)	Darlington	L	1-2	Gee	3,585

FINAL LEAGUE POSITION : 3rd in Division Three

Appearances

Sub. Appearances

Goals

Wallington	Streete	Buckley	Lewis	Hindmarch	MacLaren	Micklewhite	Christie	Davison	McClaren	Chandler	Blades	Palmer	Williams	Garner	Harbey	Gregory	Pratley	Gee	Steele	Thomas	#
1	2	3	4	5	6	7	8	9	10	11											1
1	2	3	4*	5	6	7	8	9	10	11	12										2
1	2	3	4	5	6	7	8	9	10*	11	12										3
1	2	3	4	5	6	7	8	9	10	11*	12										4
1	2	3	4	5	6	7	8	9	10	11											5
1		3		5	6	7	8	9	10*	11	12	2	4								6
1		3		5	6	7	8	9	10	11		2	4								7
1		3		5	6	7	8	9	10	11		2	4								8
1		3		5	6	7	8	9	10*	11	12	2	4								9
1		3		5	6	7	8	9	10	11		2	4								10
1		3		5	6	7	8	9	10*	11		2	4	12							11
1		3		5	6	7	8*	9	10	11		2	4	12							12
1		3		5	6	7		9	10	11		2	4	8							13
1		3		5	6	7	8	9	10*	11		2	4	12							14
1		3		5	6	7	8	9	10	11	12	2*	4								15
1		3		5	6	7	8	9		11		2	4	10							16
1		3		5	6	7	8	9*		11		2	4	10	12						17
1		3		5	6	7	8	9		11*		2	4	12		10					18
1		3		5	6	7	8	9*		11		2	4	12		10					19
1		3		5	6	7	8	9		11		2	4	10							20
1		3		5	6	7	8	9		11*		2	4	12		10					21
1		3		5	6	7	8	9		11		2	4			10					22
1		3		5	6	7	8			11		2	4	9		10					23
1		3			6	7	8			11		2	4	9		10	5				24
1		3			6	7	8			11*		2	4	9	12	10	5				25
1		3		5	6	7	8	9		11		2	4	9		10					26
1		3		5	6	7	8	9		11		2	4			10					27
1		3		5	6	7	8	9		11		2	4			10					28
1		3		5	6	7	8			11		2	4			10	9				29
		3		5	6	7	8	9		11		2	4			10			1		30
		3			6	7	8	9		11		2	4			10	5		1		31
		3			6	7	8	9		11		2	4			10	5		1		32
		3		5*	6	7	8	9				2	4	12		10			1	11	33
		3			6	7	8	9	12			2	4			10*	5		1	11	34
		3		5	6	7	8	9	10			2	4						1	11	35
		3			6	7	8	9	10			2	4				5		1	11	36
		3			6	7	8	9	10			2	4	12			5		1	11*	37
		3		5	6	7	8	9	10			2*	4	12					1	11	38
		3		5	6	7	8	9	10			2	4						1	11	39
		3		5	6	7	8	9	10			2	4						1	11	40
		3		5	6	7	8	9	4			2	12			10			1	11*	41
		3		5	6	7	8	9		11		2	4			10			1		42
1		3		5	6	7	8	9*		11		2	4			10	12				43
1		3		5	6	7	8	9		11		2	4			10					44
1		3		5	6	7	8	9		11		2	4*			10	12				45
1		3*		5	6	7	8	9		12	4	2				10	11				46
33	5	46	5	39	46	46	45	41	22	36	24	18	39	8		22	7	2	13	9	
									1	1	6			1	8	3		2			
		1	1	6	4	11	15	17		9			4	5		4	2				

49

1986-87

#	Month	Date		Opponent	Result	Score	Scorers	Attendance
1	Aug	23	(h)	Oldham A	L	0-1		13,632
2		30	(a)	Birmingham C	D	1-1	Gregory	12,209
3	Sep	6	(h)	Crystal Palace	W	1-0	Gregory (pen)	12,058
4		13	(a)	Grimsby T	W	1-0	Davison	7,305
5		20	(h)	Millwall	D	1-1	Davison	12,072
6		27	(a)	West Brom A	L	0-2		10,847
7	Oct	1	(h)	Sunderland	W	3-2	Forsyth, Davison, Sage	12,448
8		4	(a)	Huddersfield T	L	0-2		7,690
9		11	(h)	Hull C	D	1-1	Gee	12,348
10		18	(a)	Shrewsbury T	W	1-0	Gee	5,714
11		21	(a)	Portsmouth	L	1-2	Gregory	9,131
12		25	(h)	Brighton & HA	W	4-1	Gee 2, Gregory, Sage	10,768
13	Nov	1	(a)	Stoke C	W	2-0	Williams, Gee	12,309
14		8	(h)	Ipswich T	W	2-1	Micklewhite, Davison	14,145
15		15	(a)	Barnsley	W	1-0	Gee	3,283
16		22	(h)	Sheffield U	W	2-0	Micklewhite, Gregory	18,092
17		29	(a)	Leeds U	L	0-2		19,129
18	Dec	6	(h)	Reading	W	3-0	Davison 3	12,695
19		13	(a)	Plymouth A	D	1-1	Micklewhite	15,812
20		21	(h)	Grimsby T	W	4-0	Micklewhite, Davison 2, Gee	14,440
21		26	(a)	Bradford C	W	1-0	Gregory (pen)	14,502
22		27	(h)	Barnsley	W	3-2	Gree, Gregory, Davison	17,574
23	Jan	3	(a)	Crystal Palace	L	0-1		9,526
24		24	(a)	Oldham A	W	4-1	Davison, Gregory (pen), Gee, Micklewhite	9,540
25	Feb	7	(h)	Brimingham C	D	2-2	Gee 2	16,834
26		14	(a)	Sunderland	W	2-1	Gregory, Davison	16,005
27		21	(h)	West Brom A	D	1-1	Gregory	16,237
28		28	(a)	Millwall	W	1-0	Callaghan	7,169
29	Mar	4	(h)	Portsmouth	D	0-0		21,085
30		7	(a)	Brighton & HA	W	1-0	Gee	9,100
31		14	(h)	Shrewsbury T	W	3-1	Callaghan, Davison 2	14,393
32		18	(h)	Blackburn R	W	3-2	Davison 2, Keeley (og)	15,076
33		21	(a)	Hull C	D	1-1	Hindmarch	9,684
34	Apr	4	(a)	Ipswich T	W	2-0	Callaghan, Davison	16,533
35		8	(h)	Huddersfield T	W	2-0	Gregory, Gee	15,432
36		11	(h)	Stoke C	D	0-0		19,038
37		17	(a)	Blackburn R	L	1-3	Hindmarch	13,019
38		20	(h)	Bradford C	W	1-0	Lillis	17,274
39		25	(a)	Sheffield U	W	1-0	Gee	19,166
40	May	2	(h)	Leeds U	W	2-1	Gee, Davison	20,087
41		4	(a)	Reading	L	0-2		9,199
42		9	(h)	Plymouth A	W	4-2	Davison, Callaghan, Micklewhite, Gregory	20,798

FINAL LEAGUE POSITION : 1st in Division Two

Appearances

Sub. Appearances

Goals

Wallington	Sage	Forsyth	Gregory	Pratley	MacLaren	Micklewhite	Lillis	Davison	Cross	Chandler	Gee	Williams	Garner	Penney	Hindmarch	Harbey	Callaghan	Blades	Steele	#
1	2	3	4	5	6	7	8	9	10	11*	12									1
1	2	3	10	5	6	7	8	9		11		4								2
1	2	3	10	5	6	7	8*	9		11	12	4								3
1	2	3	10	5	6	7		9		11	8	4								4
1	2	3	10	5	6	7		9		11	8	4								5
1	2	3	10	5	6	7		9	12	11	8*	4								6
1	2	3	10	5	6	7		9		11	8	4								7
1	2	3	10	5	6	7		9		11	8*	4	12							8
1	2	3	10	5	6	7		9		11	8*	4		12						9
1	2	3	10		6	7		9	12		8*	4			5	11				10
1	2	3	10		6	7		9			8	4			5	11				11
1	2	3	10		6	7		9*			8	4	12		5	11				12
1	2	3	10		6	7		9			8	4			5	11				13
1	2	3	10		6	7		9			8	4			5	11				14
1	2	3	10		6	7		9	11		8	4			5					15
1	2	3	10		6	7		9			8	4			5	11				16
1	2	3	10		6	7		9	12		8	4			5	11*				17
1	2	3	10		6	7	12	9			8*	4			5	11				18
1	2	3	10		6	7	12	9			8*	4			5	11				19
1	2	3	10*		6	7	12	9			8	4			5	11				20
1	2	3	10		6	7		9			8	4			5	11				21
1	2	3	10		6	7		9			8	4			5	11				22
1	2	3	10		6	7	12	9			8	4			5	11*				23
1	2		10		6	7		9	11		8	4			5	3				24
1	2	3	10		6	7	4	9			8				5		11			25
1	2*	3	10		6	7	12	9			8	4			5		11			26
1		3	10		6	7		9			8	4			5		11	2		27
1		3	10		6	7		9			8	4			5		11	2		28
1		3	10		6	7		9			8	4			5		11	2		29
1		3	10		6	7		9			8	4			5		11	2		30
1		3	10		6	7		9			8	4			5		11	2		31
1		3	10		6	7		9			8	4			5		11	2		32
1		3	10		6	7		9			8	4			5		11	2		33
1		3	10		6	7		9			8	4			5		11	2		34
		3	10		6	7		9			8	4			5		11	2	1	35
		3	10		6	7		9			8	4			5		11	2	1	36
		3	10		6	7	12	9*			8	4			5		11	2	1	37
		3	10		6	7	9				8	4			5		11	2	1	38
		3	10		6	7	9				8	4			5		11	2	1	39
		3	10		6	7		9			8	4			5		11	2	1	40
		3*	10		6	7	12	9			8	4			5		11	2	1	41
		3	10		6	7	12	9			8*	4			5		11	2	1	42
34	26	41	42	9	42	42	6	40	3	9	39	40			33	14	18	16	8	
							8		3		2		2	1						
	2	1	12			6	1	19			15	1			2		4			

51

1987-88

1	Aug	15	(h)	Luton T	W	1-0	Gregory	17,204
2		19	(a)	QPR	D	1-1	Gee	11,651
3		29	(h)	Wimbledon	L	0-1		15,165
4	Sep	5	(h)	Portsmouth	D	0-0		15,071
5		12	(a)	Norwich C	W	2-1	Davison, Gregory (pen)	14,402
6		19	(h)	Sheffield W	D	2-2	Gregory, Forsyth	15,869
7		26	(h)	Oxford U	L	0-1		15,711
8		29	(a)	Liverpool	L	0-4		43,405
9	Oct	3	(a)	West Ham U	D	1-1	Gee	17,226
10		10	(h)	Nottingham F	L	0-1		22,394
11		17	(a)	Charlton A	W	1-0	Cross	5,432
12		24	(a)	Arsenal	L	1-2	Garner	32,374
13		31	(h)	Coventry C	W	2-0	Garner 2	15,738
14	Nov	14	(a)	Newcastle U	D	0-0		21,698
15		22	(h)	Chelsea	W	2-0	Cross, Gregory	18,644
16		28	(a)	Southampton	W	2-1	Gee, Garner	15,201
17	Dec	5	(h)	Watford	D	1-1	Wright	14,516
18		12	(a)	Everton	L	0-3		26,224
19		20	(h)	Tottenham H	L	1-2	Gregory	17,593
20		26	(h)	Norwich C	L	1-2	Wright	15,452
21		28	(a)	Sheffield W	L	1-2	Gee	26,191
22	Jan	1	(a)	Wimbledon	L	1-2	Callaghan	5,479
23		16	(a)	Luton T	L	0-1		7,175
24	Feb	6	(a)	Portsmouth	L	1-2	Wright	14,790
25		10	(h)	Manchester U	L	1-2	McMinn	20,016
26		20	(a)	Oxford U	D	0-0		8,924
27		27	(h)	West Ham U	W	1-0	Callaghan	16,301
28	Mar	1	(a)	Tottenham H	D	0-0		15,986
29		5	(h)	Charlton A	D	1-1	Callaghan (pen)	16,139
30		16	(h)	Liverpool	D	1-1	Forsyth	26,356
31		19	(a)	Coventry C	W	3-0	Forsyth, Gee, Williams	19,871
32		26	(h)	Arsenal	D	0-0		18,382
33		30	(a)	Nottingham F	L	1-2	Foster (og)	25,017
34	Apr	2	(a)	Manchester U	L	1-4	Cross	40,146
35		4	(h)	Newcastle U	W	2-1	Gee, Micklewhite	18,591
36		9	(a)	Chelsea	L	0-1		16,996
37		13	(h)	QPR	L	0-2		14,214
38		23	(h)	Southampton	W	2-0	Gregory, Stapleton	14,291
39		30	(a)	Watford	D	1-1	Callaghan	14,181
40	May	2	(h)	Everton	D	0-0		17,974

FINAL LEAGUE POSITION : 15th in Division One

Appearances

Sub. Appearances

Goals

Football appearances / team-sheet grid.

Shilton	Sage	Forsyth	Williams	Hindmarch	MacLaren	Micklewhite	Gee	Davison	Gregory	Callaghan	Blades	Wright	Lillis	Garner	Cross	Lewis	Penney	McClaren	McCord	McMinn	Stapleton	#
1	2	3	4	5	6	7	8	9	10	11												1
1	2	3	4	5	6	7	8	9	10	11												2
1	2	3	4	5*		7	8	9†	10	11	12	6	14									3
1	2	3	4		6	7	8*	9	10	11		5		12								4
1	2	3	4		6	7	8*	9	10	11		5		12								5
1	7	3	4		6		8*	9	10	11	2	5		12								6
1	7	3	4		6		8†	9*	10	11	2	5		12	14							7
1	7	3	4		6		8*	9	10	11	2	5		12								8
1	2	3	4		6		8	9	10	7		5		11								9
1	2*	3	4	12			8		10	7	6	5		9	11							10
1		3	4	2				9	10	7	6	5		8	11							11
1		3	4	2			12	9	10†	7	6	5		8*	11	14						12
1		3	4	2				9	10	7	6	5		8	11							13
1		3	4	2			12	9	10	7	6	5		8*	11							14
1		3	4	2				9	10	7	6	5		8	11							15
1		3	4	2				9	10†	7	6	5		8	11*	14	12					16
1		3	4	2				9*	10†	7	6	5		8	11	14	12					17
1		3	4	2				9		7*	6	5		8	11	10†	12	14				18
1		3	4	2				9†	10	7	6	5		8	11*	14	12					19
1		3	4	2				9	10	7	6	5		8		11						20
1	12	3	4	2				9	10	7	6	5		8*		14	11†					21
1		3	4	2				9	10	7	6	5			8			11				22
1		3	4	2			8		10	7	6	5		9			11					23
1		3	4	2			8		10†	11	6	5		9*		14	12				7	24
1		3	4		6	2	9*		10	11†		5		14	8		12				7	25
1		3	4		6		9		10	11	2	5			8						7	26
1		3	4		6	14	9		10	11	2†	5		12	8*						7	27
1		3	4		6	14	9		10†	11	2	5		12	8						7*	28
1		3	4		6		9		10	11	2	5		12	8*						7	29
1		3	4		6	12	9		10	11	2	5		14	8†						7*	30
1†		3	4		6	14	12	9	10	11	2	5			8						7*	31
1		3	4		6	12	9*		10	11	2	5			8						7	32
1		3	4		6†	14	12	9	10	11	2	5			8*						7	33
1		3	4		6		7	9*	10	11	2	5		12						8		34
1		3	4		6	12	7	9	10	11	2*	5								8		35
1		3	4		6	12	7	9†	10	11	2*	5		14						8		36
1		3	4		6	12	7†	9	10	11	2*	5		14						8		37
1	3		4		6	2	7	9	10	11		5								8		38
1	2*	3	4		6	12	7	9	10	11		5								8		39
1		3	4		6	2	7	9	10	11		5								8		40
40	12	39	40	19	25	12	36	13	39	40	30	38		14	11	10	3	1	1	7	10	
	1			9	4	2			1					1	10	4	6	6	1			
		3	1				1	6	1	6	4			3	4	3				1	1	

1988-89

1	Aug	27	(h)	Middlesbrough	W	1-0	Goddard	19,432
2	Sep	3	(a)	Millwall	L	0-1		13,061
3		10	(h)	Newcastle U	W	2-0	Hebberd, Goddard	16,014
4		17	(a)	Nottingham F	D	1-1	Hebberd	24,818
5		24	(h)	QPR	L	0-1		14,008
6	Oct	1	(a)	Southampton	D	0-0		13,283
7		8	(h)	Norwich C	L	0-1		14,117
8		22	(h)	Charlton A	D	0-0		14,106
9		29	(h)	Wimbledon	W	4-1	Saunders 2, Sage, Micklewhite	15,050
10	Nov	5	(a)	Tottenham H	W	3-1	McMinn 2, Saunders	22,868
11		12	(h)	Manchester U	D	2-2	Saunders, Hebberd	24,080
12		19	(a)	Aston Villa	W	2-1	Saunders, Goddard	23,489
13		26	(h)	Arsenal	W	2-1	Callaghan, Gee	21,209
14	Dec	3	(a)	Sheffield W	D	1-1	Callaghan (pen)	20,609
15		10	(h)	Luton T	L	0-1		15,228
16		17	(a)	Coventry C	W	2-0	Saunders, McMinn	17,229
17		26	(h)	Liverpool	L	0-1		25,213
18		31	(h)	Millwall	L	0-1		16,154
19	Jan	2	(a)	Newcastle U	W	1-0	Wright	30,555
20		14	(h)	West Ham U	L	1-2	Saunders	16,796
21		21	(a)	QPR	W	1-0	Williams	9,516
22	Feb	4	(h)	Southampton	W	3-1	Hebberd, Goddard, Saunders (pen)	13,758
23		11	(a)	Norwich C	L	0-1		17,227
24		25	(h)	Everton	W	3-2	Saunders, Goddard 2	17,103
25	Mar	1	(a)	Wimbledon	L	0-4		4,207
26		11	(h)	Tottenham H	D	1-1	Saunders	18,206
27		18	(a)	Middlesbrough	W	1-0	McMinn	16,580
28		25	(h)	Nottingham F	L	0-2		25,174
29		29	(a)	Liverpool	L	0-1		42,518
30	Apr	1	(h)	Coventry C	W	1-0	Blades	15,175
31		8	(a)	West Ham U	D	1-1	Micklewhite	16,560
32		15	(a)	Manchester U	W	2-0	Micklewhite, Goddard	34,145
33		22	(h)	Sheffield W	W	1-0	Saunders	17,529
34		29	(a)	Luton T	L	0-3		8,507
35	May	6	(h)	Aston Villa	W	2-1	Saunders, Hebberd	18,112
36		10	(a)	Charlton A	L	0-3		7,448
37		13	(a)	Arsenal	W	2-1	Saunders 2 (1 pen)	41,008
38		15	(a)	Everton	L	0-1		17,826

FINAL LEAGUE POSITION : 5th in Division One

Appearances

Sub. Appearances

Goals

Shilton	Sage	Forsyth	Williams	Wright	Blades	Micklewhite	Chiedozie	Goddard	Hebberd	Callaghan	Gee	Pickering	McMinn	Cross	Penney	Hindmarch	Saunders	Patterson	#
1	2	3	4	5	6	7	8	9	10	11									1
1	2	3	4	5	6	7†	8*	9	10	11	12	14							2
1	2	3	4	5	6			9	10	11	8*	14	7†	12					3
1	2	3	4	5	6			9	10	11	8*		7	12					4
1	2	3	4	5	6	12		9	10	11		14	7*	8†					5
1	2	3	4	5	6			9	10			11	7		8				6
1	2	3	4	5	6			9	10			11	7		8				7
1	2	3	4		6			9	10			11	7		8	5			8
1	2	3	4		6	12		9	10	11*			7			5	8		9
1	2	3		5	6			9	10	11			7	4			8		10
1	2	3	4	5	6	12		9	10	11*			7				8		11
1	2	3	4	5	6	12		9	10	11*			7				8		12
1	2	3	4	5	6				10	11	9		7				8		13
1	2	3	4	5	6	12			10	11	9*		7				8		14
1		3	4	5	6			9*	10	11	12		7				8	2	15
1		3	4	5	2			9	10	11			7			6	8		16
1		3	4	5	2	12		9*	10	11†			7	14		6	8		17
1		3	4	5	2	12		9	10†	11*			7	14		6	8		18
1		3	4	5	2			9	10	11			7			6	8		19
1		3	4	5	2				10	11*	9*		7†	14	12	6	8		20
1		3	4	5	2				10	11*	9		7		12	6	8		21
1		3	4		6	11		9	10				7	2		5	8		22
1		3	4	5	2	11		9	10†				7	14	12	6	8*		23
1		3	4	5	2	7		9	10	11						6	8		24
1		3	4	5	2	7†		9	10*	11				14	12	6	8		25
1		3	4	5	2	11		9*	10				7	12		6	8		26
1		3	4	5	2	11		9	10				7			6	8		27
1		3	4	5	2	11		9*	10				7	12		6	8		28
1		3	4	5	2	11			10*		9		7	12		6	8		29
1		3	4	5	2	11		9	10				7			6	8		30
1		3	4	5	2	11		9*	10				7	12		6	8		31
1		3	4	5	2	11		9	10				7			6	8		32
1		3	4	5	2	11		9	10				7			6	8		33
1		3	4	5	2	11		9†	10*		12		7	14		6	8		34
1		3	4	5	2	11		9	10				7			6	8		35
1		3	4	5	2	11		9	10				7*	12		6	8		36
1	2	3	4		5	11		9	10				7			6	8		37
1	2	3	4		5	11*		9†	10			14	7	12		6	8		38
38	16	38	37	33	38	19	2	31	37	18	8	5	32	7	3	25	30	1	
						7					4	3		12	6				
	1		1	1	1	3		7	5	2	1	4	14						

1989-90

1	Aug	19	(a)	Charlton A	D	0-0		8,543
2		23	(h)	Wimbledon	D	1-1	Hebberd	13,874
3		26	(h)	Manchester U	W	2-0	Goddard, Saunders (pen)	22,175
4		30	(a)	Nottingham F	L	1-2	Hodge (og)	24,060
5	Sep	9	(h)	Liverpool	L	0-3		20,034
6		16	(a)	QPR	W	1-0	Saunders	10,697
7		23	(h)	Southampton	L	0-1		13,694
8		30	(a)	Aston Villa	L	0-1		16,245
9	Oct	14	(h)	Crystal Palace	W	3-1	Goddard 2, Saunders (pen)	14,535
10		21	(h)	Chelsea	L	0-1		12,279
11		28	(a)	Arsenal	D	1-1	Goddard	33,189
12	Nov	4	(a)	Luton T	L	0-1		8,919
13		11	(h)	Manchester C	W	6-0	Wright, Hebberd, Saunders 2 (2 pens), Goddard, Micklewhite	19,239
14		18	(h)	Sheffield W	W	2-0	Goddard, Saunders	18,085
15		25	(a)	Tottenham H	W	2-1	Saunders, Goddard	28,075
16	Dec	2	(h)	Charlton A	W	2-0	Saunders, Micklewhite	14,590
17		9	(a)	Wimbledon	D	1-1	Goddard	5,024
18		16	(a)	Norwich C	L	0-1		16,184
19		26	(h)	Everton	L	0-1		21,314
20		30	(h)	Coventry C	W	4-1	Pickering, Hebberd 2, Ramage	17,011
21	Jan	1	(a)	Millwall	D	1-1	Pickering	12,790
22		13	(a)	Manchester U	W	2-1	Wright, Pickering	38,985
23		20	(h)	Nottingham F	L	0-2		24,176
24	Feb	10	(h)	QPR	W	2-0	Gee, Saunders	14,445
25		24	(h)	Tottenham H	W	2-1	Saunders, Harford	19,676
26	Mar	3	(a)	Sheffield W	L	0-1		21,811
27		10	(a)	Southampton	L	1-2	Saunders	16,430
28		17	(h)	Aston Villa	L	0-1		21,062
29		20	(a)	Crystal Palace	D	1-1	Wright	10,051
30		24	(h)	Arsenal	L	1-3	Briscoe	17,514
31		31	(a)	Chelsea	D	1-1	Harford	14,265
32	Apr	7	(a)	Coventry C	L	0-1		11,157
33		14	(h)	Millwall	W	2-0	Harford 2	13,718
34		16	(a)	Everton	L	1-2	Wright	23,933
35		21	(h)	Norwich C	L	0-2		13,758
36		28	(a)	Manchester C	W	1-0	Wright	29,542
37	May	1	(a)	Liverpool	L	0-1		38,038
38		5	(h)	Luton T	L	2-3	Wright, Williams P	17,044

FINAL LEAGUE POSITION : 16th in Division One

Appearances

Sub. Appearances

Goals

Shilton	Sage	Forsyth	Williams G	Wright	Hindmarch	McMinn	Saunders	Goddard	Pickering	Micklewhite	Cross	Hebberd	Gee	Blades	Ramage	McCord	Harford	Patterson	Francis	Davidson	Briscoe	Williams P	Hayward	Taylor	
1	2	3	4	5	6	7*	8	9	10	11	12														1
1	2	3	4	5	6	7	8	9†	10*	11		12	14												2
1		3	4	5	6	7*	8	9		11	12	10		2											3
1		3	4	5	6	7*	8	9†		11	12	10	14	2											4
1		3	4	5	6	7*	8	9	12	11		10		2											5
1		3	4	5	6	7	8	9		11		10		2											6
1	12	3	4	5	6	7	8	9	10	11†			14	2*											7
1	2	3	4	5		7	8	9*		11		10	12	6											8
1	2	3	4	5		7	8	9	12	11		10		6*											9
1	2	3	4	5		7	8	9	12	11		10*		6											10
1	2	3	4	5		7	8	9	12	11		10		6*											11
1	2	3	4	5		7	8	9		11		10		6											12
1	2	3	4	5		7	8	9		11		10		6											13
1	2	3	4	5		7	8	9		11		10		6											14
1	2	3	4	5	6	7*	8	9	12	11		10													15
1	2	3	4	5	6		8		7	11		10			9										16
1	2	3	4	5	6		8	9	7	11		10													17
1	2	3	4	5	6†		8	9	7	11	12	10*	14												18
1	2	3	4	5			8	9*	7		11†	10		6	12	14									19
1	2	3	4	5*			8		7		12	10		6	9	11									20
1	2	3	4	5			8		7		12	10		6	9		11*								21
1	2	3	4	5	6		8		7	11		10			9										22
1	2	3	4	5	6		8	7†				10				14	9	11*	12						23
1	2	3	4	5			8					10	7		9					6	11				24
1	2	3	4	5	6		8		11				7*		12		9	10							25
1	2	3	4	5	6		8		11				7†		12		9*	10			14				26
1	2	3	4		5		8	11*					7†	6	12		9	10	14						27
1	2	3	4	5			8	11*					6	10†			9	7	12		14				28
1	2	3	4	5			8	11					6				9	7*		10	12				29
1	2	3	4	5	6		8	10*									9			11	7	12			30
	2	3	4	5	6		8	10*									9	14		11	7†	12	1		31
	2	3	4	5	6		8										9	12	14	11	7†	10*	1		32
1	2	3	4	5	6		8										9	7		11	10				33
	2	3	4	5	6		8										9	7*	12	11	10		1		34
1	2	3	4	5†	6		8										9	7*	12	14	11	10			35
1	2	3	4	5	6		8							11			9			7		10			36
1	2	3	4	5	6		8							11*			9		12	7		10			37
1	2	3	4	5	6		8				12			11*			9			7		10			38
35	33	38	38	36	26	15	38	18	18	18	2	21	4	18	8	2	16	9		4	8	9	1	3	
	1								5		6	2	4	1	4	2		8	2	2	1	2			
			6				11	8	3	2		4	1		1		4			1	1				

1990-91

#		Date		Venue	Opponent	Result		Scorers	Attendance
1	Aug	25	(a)	Chelsea	L	1-2	Saunders		24,652
2		29	(h)	Sheffield U	D	1-1	Saunders		18,011
3	Sep	1	(h)	Wimbledon	D	1-1	Saunders (pen)		12,469
4		8	(a)	Tottenham H	L	0-3			29,614
5		15	(h)	Aston Villa	L	0-2			19,024
6		22	(a)	Norwich C	L	1-2	Patterson		13,258
7		29	(h)	Crystal Palace	L	0-2			15,202
8	Oct	6	(a)	Liverpool	L	0-2			37,076
9		20	(h)	Manchester C	D	1-1	Saunders		17,884
10		27	(a)	Southampton	W	1-0	Harford		16,328
11	Nov	3	(h)	Luton T	W	2-1	Saunders (pen), Callaghan		15,008
12		10	(h)	Manchester U	D	0-0			21,115
13		17	(a)	Leeds U	L	0-3			27,868
14		24	(h)	Nottingham F	W	2-1	Ramage, Saunders		21,729
15	Dec	1	(a)	Sunderland	W	2-1	Saunders, Harford		21,212
16		15	(h)	Chelsea	L	4-6	Saunders 2, Hebberd, Micklewhite		15,057
17		23	(h)	QPR	D	1-1	Saunders		16,429
18		26	(a)	Arsenal	L	0-3			25,538
19		29	(a)	Everton	L	0-2			25,361
20	Jan	1	(h)	Coventry C	D	1-1	Harford		15,741
21		12	(a)	Wimbledon	L	1-3	Harford		4,724
22		20	(h)	Tottenham H	L	0-1			17,747
23		26	(a)	Sheffield U	L	0-1			18,390
24	Feb	2	(a)	Aston Villa	L	2-3	Harford, Sage		21,852
25		23	(h)	Norwich C	D	0-0			14,102
26	Mar	2	(h)	Sunderland	D	3-3	Saunders 3 (1 pen)		16,027
27		16	(a)	Crystal Palace	L	1-2	Micklewhite		14,752
28		23	(h)	Liverpool	L	1-7	Saunders (pen)		20,531
29		30	(h)	Arsenal	L	0-2			18,397
30	Apr	1	(a)	QPR	D	1-1	Harford		12,036
31		10	(a)	Nottingham F	L	0-1			25,109
32		13	(a)	Coventry	L	0-3			11,961
33		16	(a)	Manchester U	L	1-3	Williams P		32,776
34		20	(a)	Manchester C	L	1-2	Harford		24,037
35		23	(h)	Leeds U	L	0-1			12,666
36	May	4	(h)	Southampton	W	6-2	Williams P 3 (1 pen), Saunders 2, Phillips		11,680
37		8	(h)	Everton	L	2-3	Harford (pen), Saunders		12,403
38		11	(a)	Luton T	L	0-2			12,889

FINAL LEAGUE POSITION : 20th in Division One

Appearances

Sub. Appearances

Goals

Shilton	Sage	Forsyth	Williams G	Wright	Davidson	Micklewhite	Saunders	Harford	Ramage	Williams P	Patterson	Hebberd	Watson	Francis	Callaghan	Cross	Gee	Pickering	Briscoe	Kavanagh	Taylor	McMinn	Wilson	Phillips	Hayward	No.
1	2	3	4	5	6	7	8	9	10	11*	12															1
1	2	3	4	5		7	8	9	6	11		10														2
1	2	3	4	5		7*	8	9	10†	11		12	6	14												3
1	2	3	4	5		7*	8	9	10†	11	14	12	6													4
1		3	4	5		7	8	9		11	2	10	6													5
1	12	3	4	5	11	7†	8	9			2*	10	6	14												6
1	2	3	4	5		7*	8	9		10		12	6		11											7
1	2	6	4	5		7	8	9	10	3					11											8
1	2	6	4	5		7	8	9	10*			12			11	3										9
1	2	6	4	5		7	8	9	10						11	3										10
1	2	6	4	5		7	8		10						11	3	9									11
1	2*	6	4	5		7	8	9	10						11	3		12								12
1		6	4	5		7	8	9	10*		14	12			11	3†		2								13
1		6	4*	5		7	8	9	12		3	10			11			2								14
1		6		5			8	9	4		2	10			11			3	7							15
1	2	6		5		7	8	9	4*	12		10			11			3								16
1	2	6		5		7	8	9	12	4†		10*			11			3		14						17
	2	6		5	12	7*	8	9	10	4†					11			3		14	1					18
	2	6		5		7†	8	9	10*	4						11	12	3		14	1					19
	2	6		5	12		8	9	10	4*						11		3		7	1					20
1	2			5	12		8	9		4	10					7		3*	11	6						21
1	2		4	5		7*	8	9		12	10					3		11		6						22
1	2	6	4	5		7	8	9				10				3						11				23
1	2	6	4	5		7	8	9				10				3						11				24
1	2	6	4	5		7	8	9				12				3						11*	10			25
1	2	6	4	5		7	8	9								3						11	10			26
1	2	6	4	5		7	8					11				3						9	10			27
1	2	6	4	5		7	8	9				12				3						11	10*			28
1	2	6	4	5		7	8	9								3						11	10			29
1	2	6	4	5		7	8	9								3		11					10			30
1	2	6	4	5†		7	8	9		12						3				14		11*	10			31
1	2	6	4	5		7	8	9					.			3						11	10			32
	2	6	4	5		7	8	9		11									3		1		10			33
	2		4	5		7	8	9		11	12					14		3	6†		1		10*			34
	2	3*	4	5		7†	8	9	10		12									14	1	11		6		35
1	2	3	4	5*		7	8	9	10		12											11		6		36
	2	5	4			7†	8	9	10									12			1	11	3*	6	14	37
1	2	3	4	5		7	8	9	10*	6		12			14							11†				38
31	33	35	31	37	2	35	38	36	15	17	6	12	5		12	19	1	12	2	5	7	13	11	3		
	1				3				2	2	5	9		2		2	1	1	1	6				1		
	1					2	17	8	1	4	1	1			1	1							1			

59

1991-92

1	Aug	17	(a)	Sunderland	D	1-1	Harford	20,509
2		21	(h)	Middlesbrough	W	2-0	Comyn, Harford	12,805
3		24	(h)	Southend U	L	1-2	Williams P	12,284
4	Sep	1	(a)	Charlton A	W	2-0	Williams P, Harford	6,602
5		4	(h)	Blackburn R	L	0-2		12,078
6		7	(h)	Barnsley	D	1-1	Williams P	10,559
7		13	(a)	Cambridge U	D	0-0		7,293
8		18	(a)	Oxford U	L	0-2		4,319
9		21	(h)	Brighton & HA	W	3-1	Davison, Patterson, Williams P (pen)	12,004
10		28	(a)	Newcastle U	D	2-2	Davison, Ormondroyd	17,581
11	Oct	5	(h)	Bristol C	W	4-1	Aizlewood (og), Micklewhite, Davison 2	11,880
12		12	(a)	Swindon T	W	2-1	Williams P, Gee	11,883
13		19	(h)	Portsmouth	W	2-0	McMinn, Williams P	13,190
14		26	(a)	Millwall	W	2-1	Davison, Ormondroyd	7,660
15	Nov	2	(h)	Tranmere R	L	0-1		11,501
16		6	(a)	Port Vale	L	0-1		8,589
17		9	(a)	Wolverhampton W	W	3-2	Davison, Ormondroyd, Bennett (og)	15,672
18		16	(h)	Ipswich T	W	1-0	Davison	12,493
19		23	(a)	Bristol R	W	3-2	Patterson, Williams P (pen), Davison	6,513
20		30	(h)	Leicester C	L	1-2	Ormondroyd	19,306
21	Dec	7	(a)	Watford	W	2-1	Ormondroyd 2	8,302
22		26	(h)	Grimsby T	D	0-0		16,392
23		28	(h)	Charlton A	L	1-2	Ormondroyd	14,367
24	Jan	1	(a)	Middlesbrough	D	1-1	Chalk	16,288
25		11	(a)	Southend U	L	0-1		8,295
26		18	(h)	Sunderland	L	1-2	Williams G	15,384
27	Feb	1	(a)	Portsmouth	W	1-0	Gabbiadini	12,008
28		8	(h)	Millwall	L	0-2		12,773
29		11	(a)	Blackburn R	L	0-2		15,350
30		15	(h)	Bristol R	W	1-0	Coleman	11,154
31		22	(a)	Leicester C	W	2-1	Ormondroyd, Simpson	18,148
32		29	(h)	Watford	W	3-1	Williams P 3 (1 pen)	14,052
33	Mar	7	(a)	Plymouth A	D	1-1	Simpson	8,864
34		11	(h)	Port Vale	W	3-1	Williams G, Simpson, Gabbiadini	14,983
35		14	(a)	Tranmere R	L	3-4	Kitson, Coleman, Simpson	10,386
36		21	(h)	Wolverhampton W	L	1-2	Kitson	21,024
37		24	(h)	Plymouth A	W	2-0	Johnson, McMinn	13,799
38		28	(a)	Ipswich T	L	1-2	Simpson	15,305
39	Apr	1	(h)	Cambridge U	D	0-0		15,353
40		4	(a)	Barnsley	W	3-0	Simpson, Forsyth, Williams P (pen)	10,121
41		7	(a)	Grimsby T	W	1-0	Gabbiadini	7,040
42		11	(h)	Oxford U	D	2-2	Simpson, Williams P (pen)	15,555
43		15	(a)	Brighton & HA	W	2-1	Gabbiadini 2	8,159
44		20	(h)	Newcastle U	W	4-1	Williams P (pen), Kitson, Ramage 2	21,363
45		25	(a)	Bristol C	W	2-1	Gabbiadini, Micklewhite	16,648
46	May	2	(h)	Swindon T	W	2-1	Kitson, Johnson	22,608

FINAL LEAGUE POSITION : 3rd in Division Two

Appearances

Sub. Appearances

Goals

Shilton	Sage	Forsyth	Williams G	Coleman	Comyn	Micklewhite	Gee	Harford	Williams P	McMinn	Cross	Pickering	Taylor	Hayward	Ramage	Patterson	Stallard	Ormondroyd	Davison	Kavanagh	Chalk	Davidson	Sturridge	Gabbiadini	Simpson	Round	Kitson	Johnson	—	
1	2	3	4	5	6	7	8*	9	10	11	12																			1
1	2	3	4	5	6	7	8	9	10	11																				2
1	2	3	4	5	6	7	8*	9	10	11	12																			3
	2	3	4	5	6	7	8	9	10	11*	12	1																		4
1	2	3	4	5	6	7†	8*	9	10	11	12			14																5
1	2	3	4	5	6	7	8	9	10	11*	12																			6
1	2	3	4	5	6	7	8		10	11				12	9*															7
1	2	3	4	5	6	7	8†		10*	11				9		12	14													8
1	2	3	4	5	6	7*			10	11						12	8	9												9
1	2*	3	4	5	6	7			10	11						12	8	9												10
1	2	3	4	5	6	7			10	11							8	9												11
1		3	4	5	6	7	9		10	11						2	8													12
1	2	3	4	5	6	7	9		10	11							8													13
1	2	3	4	5	6	7			10	11							8	9												14
1	2	3	4	5	6	7	11*		10							12	8	9												15
1	2	3	4	5	6	7	11		10								8	9												16
1	2	3	4	5	6	7	11		10								8	9												17
1	2*	3	4	5	6	7			10	11				12			8	9												18
1		3*	4		6	7	12		10	11				5†		2	8	9		14										19
1			4	5	6	7			10	11						2	8	9		3										20
1		3	4	5	6	7	9		10	11						2	8													21
1		3	4	5	6	7	9*		10	11						2	8				12									22
1		3	4	5	6	7†	9*		10	11						2	8			14	12									23
1		3	4	5	6				10	11						2	9	8			7									24
1		3†	4	5	6									12		2	9	8		14	7	10	11*							25
1		3	4	5	6	7*	9		11					10			8		2		12									26
1		3	4	5	6				10	11							8		2		7			9						27
1		3	4	5	6	12			10	11							8		2		7*			9						28
1		3	4	5	6	7			10	11							8		2					9						29
1		3	4	5	6	7	12		10	11							8		2					9*						30
1		3	4	5	6				10	7							8		2					9	11					31
1		3	4	5	6				10	7							8		2					9	11					32
			4	5	6	12			10	7*		1					8		2					9	11	3				33
			4	5	6	7			10			1							2					9	11	3	8			34
		3	4	5	6				10			1							2					9	11		8	7		35
		3	4	5	6				10	12		1							2					9	11*		8	7		36
		3	4	5	6				10*	12									2					9	11		8	7	1	37
		3	4	5	6				10										2					9	11		8	7	1	38
		3	4	5	6				10										2					9	11		8	7	1	39
		3		5	6		4		10*										2					9	11	12	8	7	1	40
		3		5	6		4								10				2					9	11		8	7	1	41
		3		5	6		4								10				2					9	11		8	7	1	42
		3		5	6	8	4								10				2					9	11			7	1	43
		3			6		4	5							10				2					9	11		8	7	1	44
		3			6	12	4	5							10				2					9	11		8*	7	1	45
		3		5	6	12	4								10				2					9*	11		8	7	1	46
31	17	43	39	43	46	28	17	6	41	35		5	3	7	8	2	25	10	22	4	1	1		20	16	2	12	12	10	
						4	2		2	4	1			4		4	1	3	3					1						
	1	2	2	1	2	1	3	13	2					2	2			8	8	1				6	7		4	2		

61

1992-93

#	Month	Date		Opponent		Score	Scorers	Attendance
1	Aug	15	(a)	Peterborough U	L	0-1		9,955
2		22	(h)	Newcastle U	L	1-2	Pembridge	17,522
3		26	(a)	Leicester C	L	2-3	Simpson 2	17,739
4		29	(a)	Watford	D	0-0		9,809
5	Sep	6	(h)	Bristol C	L	3-4	Simpson 3	12,738
6		12	(a)	Barnsley	D	1-1	Kitson	8,412
7		20	(a)	West Ham U	D	1-1	Miklosko (og)	11,493
8		26	(h)	Southend U	W	2-0	Gabbiadini, Simpson (pen)	15,172
9	Oct	3	(a)	Cambridge U	W	3-1	Simpson 2 (1 pen), Gabbiadini	6,170
10		11	(h)	Oxford U	L	0-1		14,249
11		17	(a)	Luton T	W	3-1	Kitson 2, Johnson	8,848
12		24	(h)	Charlton A	W	4-3	Gabbiadini, Minto (og), Pembridge, Simpson	15,482
13		31	(a)	Wolverhampton W	W	2-0	Kitson, Short	17,270
14	Nov	3	(a)	Notts Co	W	2-0	Pembridge, Kitson	15,267
15		7	(h)	Millwall	L	1-2	Pembridge	17,087
16		14	(a)	Bristol R	W	2-1	Kitson, Johnson	6,668
17		21	(h)	Sunderland	L	0-1		17,581
18		28	(h)	Tranmere R	L	1-2	Kitson	15,665
19	Dec	6	(a)	Swindon T	W	4-2	Johnson, Pembridge, Kuhl, McMinn	8,924
20		12	(h)	Brimingham C	W	3-1	Johnson, Kitson, Williams	16,662
21		20	(a)	Grimsby T	W	2-0	Johnson, Kitson	6,475
22		26	(a)	Brentford	L	1-2	Kitson	10,226
23		28	(h)	Portsmouth	L	2-4	Johnson, Kitson	21,478
24	Jan	10	(h)	West Ham U	L	0-2		13,737
25		16	(a)	Southend U	D	0-0		4,243
26		31	(a)	Newcastle U	D	1-1	Johnson	27,285
27	Feb	6	(h)	Peterborough U	L	2-3	Kitson 2	16,062
28		10	(h)	Barnsley	W	3-0	Gabbiadini, Kitson, Williams	13,096
29		20	(h)	Watford	L	1-2	Pembridge (pen)	15,190
30		24	(h)	Leicester C	W	2-0	Forsyth, Gabbiadini	17,507
31		27	(a)	Oxford U	W	1-0	Williams	7,456
32	Mar	3	(h)	Cambridge U	D	0-0		14,106
33		10	(h)	Bristol R	W	3-1	Short, Williams, Gabbiadini	13,294
34		13	(a)	Millwall	L	0-1		9,365
35		21	(h)	Swindon T	W	2-1	Kitson, Pembridge (pen)	12,166
36		24	(a)	Sunderland	L	0-1		17,246
37	Apr	2	(a)	Tranmere R	L	1-2	Simpson	7,774
38		6	(a)	Birmingham C	D	1-1	Johnson	15,424
39		10	(h)	Brentford	W	3-2	Kitson, Gabbiadini, Simpson	12,366
40		12	(a)	Portsmouth	L	0-3		23,805
41		17	(h)	Grimsby T	W	2-1	Simpson, Kitson	12,428
42		20	(a)	Bristol C	D	0-0		8,869
43		24	(h)	Luton T	D	1-1	Short	13,741
44	May	1	(a)	Charlton A	L	1-2	Gabbiadini	7,802
45		5	(h)	Notts Co	W	2-0	McMinn, Pembridge (pen)	13,326
46		8	(h)	Wolverhampton W	W	2-0	Gabbiadini, Hayward	15,083

FINAL LEAGUE POSITION : 8th in Division One

Appearances

Sub. Appearances

Goals

Sutton	Kavanagh	Forsyth	Pembridge	Coleman	Wassall	Johnson	Kitson	Gabbiadini	Williams	Simpson	McMinn	Comyn	Micklewhite	Patterson	Taylor	Short	Sturridge	Kuhl	Goulooze	Hayward	Nicholson	Round	Stallard	Ramage	#
1	2	3	4	5	6	7	8*	9	10	11	12														1
1	2	3	4	5	6	7	8	9*	10	11	12														2
1	2	3	4	5	6	9	8		10	11	7														3
1	2	3	4	5	6	9†	8*	12	10	11	7	14													4
1	2	3	4	5	6	9†	8	7*	10	11		14	12												5
1		3	4*	5	6	7	8	9	10	11	12			2											6
		3	6	12	5	7	8	9†	10*	11		2			1	4	14								7
1		3	6	12	5	7	9	10	11			2				4		8*							8
1		3	6	12	5	7	9	10	11			2				4		8*	14						9
1		3	6	5	7*	9	10	11				2				4		8	12						10
1		3	6	5	7	9	10	11*			12	2				4		8							11
1		3	6†	5	7*	9	10	11			12	2				4		8	14						12
1		3	6	5	7	9	10	11				2				4		8							13
1		3	6	5	7	9*	10	11			12	2				4		8							14
1		3	6	5	7†	9*	10	11			12	2	14			4		8							15
1		3	6	5	7	9	10	11				2				4		8							16
1		3	6	5	7	9	10	11*			12	2†	14			4		8							17
1		3	6	5	7	9	10	11				2				4		8							18
1		3	6	5	7*	9	10	11			12					4		8	2						19
1	2	3	6	5	7	9	10	11								4		8							20
		3	6	5	7	9	10	11							1	4		8	2						21
1		3	6	5	7*	9	10	11			12					4		8	2						22
1		3	6	5	7	9	10	11			12		14			4		8*	2†						23
1	2	3	6	5	10*	9	12	11						7		4		8							24
1	2	3	6	5	7	9	10							11		4		8							25
1	2	3	6	5*	7	9	10				12			11		4		8							26
1	2	3	6	5	7*	9	10				12			11		4		8							27
		3	6	4		9	10	7	11			2			1	5		8							28
		3	6	4		9	10	7	11		12	2			1	5		8*							29
		3	6	11		9	10	7		8*		2			1	5			12		4				30
		3		11		9	10	7				2			1	5	6	8			4				31
		3		11*		9	10	7			12	2			1	5	6	8			4				32
		3	6	11		9	10	7				2			1	5		8			4				33
		3	6			9	10	7	11			2	·		1	5		8			4				34
		3	6	11		9	10*	7					14		1	5†		8			4	2	12		35
		3	6	5		9	10*	7	11		12				1			8			4	2			36
		3	6	12		9	10†	7*	11			2	14		1	5		8			3		4		37
		3	6				10*	7†	11			4			1	5	14	8	12		3	2	9		38
			6	4		9	10		11						1	5	7	8			3	2			39
			6†	4		9	10		11				14		1	5	7	8			3*	2	12		40
			5		6	9	10†		11			4	14		1		7*	8			3	2	12		41
		4	6			9	10		11			2			1	5	7	8			3				42
		4	6	12†		9	10		11			2			1	5	7	8*			3		14		43
		4	6			9	10		11		12	2			1	5	7*	8			3				44
		4	6			9*	10		11		12	2			1	5	7	8			3				45
			6	4			10	7	11			2			1	5	9*	8			3		12		46
25	10	41	42	17	24	34	44	42	19	32	6	13	4	17	21	38	8	32	7	6	17	6	1		
			8	1		2			3		13	4	2	1		2		5	1			4	1		
		1	8		8	17	9	4	12	2				3		1		1							

1993-94

1	Aug	14	(h)	Sunderland	W 5-0	Pembridge 2 (1 pen), Gabbiadini, Kitson, Short	18,027
2		18	(a)	Nottingham F	D 1-1	Forsyth	26,682
3		21	(a)	Middlesbrough	L 0-3		15,168
4		28	(h)	Bristol C	W 1-0	Gabbiadini	15,643
5	Sep	4	(a)	Birmingham C	L 0-3		14,582
6		11	(h)	Peterborough U	W 2-0	Gabbiadini, Johnson	14,779
7		18	(a)	Millwall	D 0-0		9,881
8		25	(a)	Notts Co	L 1-4	Gabbiadini	11,005
9	Oct	3	(h)	West Brom A	W 5-3	Kitson, Simpson 2, Pembridge (pen), Short	13,370
10		9	(h)	Luton T	W 2-1	Kitson, Johnson	15,885
11		16	(a)	Portsmouth	L 2-3	Johnson, Kitson	12,404
12		23	(h)	Crystal Palace	W 3-1	Harkes, Kitson, Pembridge	16,586
13		30	(a)	Bolton W	W 2-0	Pembridge, Simpson	11,464
14	Nov	2	(a)	Charlton Ath	W 2-1	Simpson, Pembridge	8,123
15		7	(h)	Wolves	L 0-4		14,310
16		13	(a)	Oxford U	L 0-2		7,151
17		20	(h)	Grimsby T	W 2-1	Short, Pembridge (pen)	13,498
18		27	(h)	Southend U	L 1-3	Simpson	14,458
19	Dec	5	(a)	Wolves	D 2-2	Gabbiadini 2	16,900
20		18	(a)	Sunderland	L 0-1		16,001
21		27	(a)	Barnsley	W 1-0	Kitson	11,565
22		28	(h)	Leicester C	W 3-2	Pembridge, Gabbiadini, Johnson	17,372
23	Jan	1	(a)	Stoke C	L 1-2	Gabbiadini	20,307
24		3	(h)	Tranmere R	W 4-0	Gabbiadini 3, Williams	16,874
25		15	(h)	Portsmouth	W 1-0	Johnson	15,645
26		22	(a)	Luton T	L 1-2	Forsyth	9,371
27		29	(h)	Watford	L 1-2	Kitson	15,308
28	Feb	5	(a)	Crystal Palace	D 1-1	Charles	15,615
29		12	(h)	Bolton W	W 2-0	Pembridge, Gabbiadini	16,698
30		19	(a)	Watford	W 4-3	Watson (og), Kitson, Johnson, Gabbiadini	8,277
31		22	(h)	Middlesbrough	L 0-1		14,716
32		25	(h)	Birmingham C	D 1-1	Johnson	16,624
33	Mar	5	(a)	Bristol C	D 0-0		8,723
34		12	(h)	Millwall	D 0-0		15,303
35		16	(a)	Peterborough U	D 2-2	Johnson, Nicholson	7,371
36		26	(a)	West Brom A	W 2-1	Johnson, Simpson	17,437
37		29	(a)	Tranmere R	L 0-4		7,144
38	Apr	2	(h)	Barnsley	W 2-0	Johnson, Harkes	14,968
39		5	(a)	Leicester C	D 3-3	Kitson 2, Willis (og)	20,050
40		9	(h)	Stoke C	W 4-2	Simpson, Cranson (og), Pembridge, Kitson	16,593
41		16	(h)	Charlton Ath	W 2-0	Johnson, Kitson	15,784
42		20	(h)	Notts Co	D 1-1	Dijkstra (og)	18,602
43		23	(a)	Grimsby T	D 1-1	Kitson	7,451
44		27	(h)	Nottingham F	L 0-2		19,300
45		30	(h)	Oxford U	W 2-1	Pembridge (pen), Johnson	16,206
46	May	8	(a)	Southend U	L 3-4	Simpson 2, Johnson	8,119

FINAL LEAGUE POSITION : 6th in Division One

Appearances

Sub. Appearances

Goals

Taylor	Charles	Forsyth	Kuhl	Short	Wassall	Simpson	Williams	Kitson	Gabbiadini	Pembridge	Harkes	Ramage	Johnson	Kavanagh	Coleman	Hayward	Nicholson	Ratcliffe	Cowans											
1	2	3	4	5	6	7	8	9	10	11																				1
1	2	3	4	5	6		8	9	10	11	7																			2
1	2	3	4	5	6			9†	10	11	7	8*	12	14																3
1	2	3	4	5	6		8	9	10	11	7																			4
1	2	3	4	5		11	8	9	10		7				6															5
1	2	3	4	5	6	11	8	9	10				7																	6
1	2	3	4	5	6	7	8	9	10	11																				7
1	2	3	4	5	6	7	8	9	10*	11		12																		8
1	2	3	4	5	6	7	8†	9	10*	11	14	12																		9
1		3		5	6	11		9	10	4	7	8	2																	10
1	2*	3		5	6	11		9	10†	4	7	8	12			14														11
1		3	4	5	6	11		9		10	7	8	2																	12
1	8	3	4	5	6*	11	12	9		10	7		2																	13
1	8	3	4	5	6	11		9		10	7		2																	14
1	2	3	4*	5		11	12	9		10	7		8	6																15
1	2	3		5		11	10	9			7		8	12	6†	14	4													16
1	2	3		5	6	11	12	9	10	4	7	8*																		17
1	2	3		5	6	11		9	10	4	7	8																		18
1	2	3	4	5	6	11		9	10	8	7																			19
1	2	3	4	5	6	11*	14	9	10	8†	7		12																	20
1	2	3	4	5	6		11	9*	10†	8	7	14	12																	21
1	2	3	4	5	6		11		10*	8	7	12	9																	22
1	2	3	4*	5	6	12	11		10		7	8†	9	14																23
1	2	3	4	5	6	12	11		10	8	7*		9																	24
1	2	3	4	5	6		11	9	10	8	7																			25
1	2	3	4		6	12		9	10	8			7	14			5*	11†												26
1	2	3*	4		6	12		9	10*	11	7		14				5													27
1	2		4			3		10		8		9	6				5	11	7											28
1	2		4†	5		12	6	9	10	8*			11	14			3		7											29
1	2			5		12	6	9	10	8			11			4*	3		7											30
1	2		4*	5		12	6	9	10	8			11				3		7											31
1	2		4	5			6	9	10	8			11				3		7											32
1	2		4*	5			6	9	10	8			12				3	11	7											33
1	2*			5				9	10	8	12		11	4			3	6	7											34
1	2			5				9	10		8		11	4			3	6	7											35
1	2			5		11	6	9	10*	12	4		8				3		7											36
1	2			5		11	6	9	10	12	4*		8				3		7											37
1	2			5		11	6	9		10	4		8				3		7											38
1	2			5			6	9	12	10	4		8*				3	11	7											39
1	2			5		11	6	9		10	4		8				3		7											40
1	2			5		11	6	9	12	10	4		8*				3		7											41
1	2			5		11	6	9	12	10	4		8				3		7*											42
1	2			5		11	6	9	12	10	4		8*	14			3†		7											43
1	2*			5		11	6	9	8	10	4		12			14	3†		7											44
1	2			5		11	6	9†	14	10	4		8*	12			3		7											45
1		12		5	6	11		14	10	4			8	2		9	3*		7†											46
46	43	27	27	43	25	27	30	41	33	39	31	3	31	9	2	2	22	6	19											
		1				7	4		6	2	2	2	6	10		3														
	1	2		3		9	1	13	13	11	2		13			1														

1994-95

1	Aug	13	(a)	Barnsley	L	1-2	Pembridge	8,737
2		20	(h)	Luton T	D	0-0		13,060
3		27	(a)	Millwall	L	1-4	Sturridge	8,809
4		31	(h)	Middlesbrough	L	0-1		14,659
5	Sep	3	(h)	Grimsby T	W	2-1	Charles, Pembridge	12,027
6		11	(a)	Swindon T	D	1-1	Kitson	9,054
7		13	(a)	Bristol C	W	2-0	Kitson, Carsley	8,029
8		17	(h)	Oldham Ath	W	2-1	Carsley, Short	13,746
9		25	(h)	Stoke C	W	3-0	Hodge, Gabbiadini, Charles	11,782
10	Oct	1	(a)	Bolton W	L	0-1		12,015
11		8	(h)	Watford	D	1-1	Hodge	13,413
12		16	(a)	Southend U	L	0-1		4,218
13		23	(a)	Notts Co	D	0-0		6,389
14		29	(h)	Charlton Ath	D	2-2	Short, Johnson	12,588
15	Nov	2	(h)	Reading	L	1-2	Gabbiadini	10,585
16		6	(a)	Portsmouth	W	1-0	Gabbiadini	5,507
17		12	(a)	Sheffield U	L	1-2	Simpson (pen)	15,001
18		19	(h)	Port Vale	W	2-0	Johnson 2	13,357
19		27	(a)	Wolverhampton W	W	2-0	Johnson, Stallard	22,768
20	Dec	3	(h)	Notts Co	D	0-0		14,278
21		11	(a)	Luton T	D	0-0		6,400
22		17	(h)	Barnsley	W	1-0	Johnson	13,205
23		26	(a)	Tranmere R	L	1-3	Johnson	11,581
24		31	(a)	Sunderland	D	1-1	Johnson	13,979
25	Jan	2	(h)	West Brom A	D	1-1	Trollope	16,035
26		14	(a)	Charlton Ath	W	4-3	Short, Gabbiadini 2, Stallard	9,389
27		22	(h)	Portsmouth	W	3-0	Simpson 3	11,143
28	Feb	4	(h)	Sheffield U	L	2-3	Williams, Kavanagh	15,882
29		11	(a)	Reading	L	0-1		8,834
30		21	(a)	Port Vale	L	0-1		9,387
31		26	(h)	Bolton W	W	2-1	Yates, Mills	11,003
32	Mar	4	(a)	Stoke C	D	0-0		13,462
33		7	(a)	Grimsby T	W	1-0	Pembridge	5,310
34		11	(h)	Millwall	W	3-2	Pembridge, Trollope, Gabbiadini	12,490
35		15	(h)	Burnley	W	4-0	Mills, Trollope, Simpson (pen), Gabbiadini	13,922
36		18	(a)	Middlesbrough	W	4-2	Mills 2, Pembridge Gabbiadini	18,168
37		22	(h)	Swindon T	W	3-1	Simpson (pen), Pembridge, Mills	16,839
38		25	(a)	Oldham Ath	L	0-1		7,696
39	Apr	1	(h)	Bristol C	W	3-1	Gabbiadini, Williams, Wrack	14,555
40		8	(h)	Sunderland	L	0-1		15,442
41		12	(h)	Wolverhampton W	D	3-3	Simpson 2 (1 pen), Gabbiadini	16,040
42		15	(a)	Burnley	L	1-3	Trollope	11,534
43		17	(h)	Tranmere R	W	5-0	Pembridge 2, Mills, Williams, Gabbiadini	13,957
44		22	(a)	West Brom A	D	0-0		15,265
45		29	(h)	Southend U	L	1-2	Mills	12,528
46	May	7	(a)	Watford	L	1-2	Pembridge	8,492

FINAL LEAGUE POSITION : 9th in Division One

Appearances

Sub. Appearances

Goals

Taylor	Charles	Forsyth	Hayward	Short	Williams	Cowans	Gabbiadini	Kitson	Pembridge	Simpson	Harkes	Wassall	Johnson	Nicholson	Kuhl	Kavanagh	Sturridge	Hodge	Stallard	Carsley	Davies	Sutton S	Trollope	Wrack	Sutton W	Yates	Mills	Hoult	Boden	Ashbee	Cooper	
1	2	3*	4	5	6	7†	8	9	10	11	12	14																				1
1	2	3	4	5		7	12	9	10	11			6	8*																		2
1	2	5	8		7			9†	10	11			6		3	4	12	14														3
1	2	3	5		7†			9	10	11			6			12	8	4*	14													4
1	2	3	5		7			9	10	12	11*		6				8	4														5
1	2	3		5	6	7	8	9	10									4		11												6
1	2	3		5	6	7	8	9*	10	12								4		11												7
1	2	3		5	6	7	8*	9	10	12		14						4		11†												8
1	2	3		5	6	7	8		10	12		14	9*					4		11†												9
1	2	3		5	6	7*	10	9		11†	12						8	4	14													10
1	2	3			6	7			10	11		5					8	4					9									11
1°	2	3		5	6	7			10*	12†	11	14					8	4					9		15							12
	2	3		5	6	7				11*		10		9		4	12			8							1					13
	2	3		5	6	7			10	11				9		4				8							1					14
	2	3		5	6	7			10	11				9		4				8							1					15
	2	3		5*	6	7			10	11				9		4	12			8							1					16
	2	3†			6	7			10	11		5		9		4*	12		14	8							1					17
				5	6					11	7			9	3	4				8		2	10				1					18
				5	6					11	7			9	3	4				8		2	10				1					19
				5	6					11	7			9	3	4				8		2	10				1					20
				5	6					11	7			9	3	4				8		2	10				1					21
		3			6					11*	7	5		9		4				8	12	2	10				1					22
	2				6		12			11*	7	5		9	3	4				8			10				1					23
		3†		5	6		12				7			9		4			14	8		2	10		11		1					24
				5	6					11	7*				3					8	12	2	10		4	9	1					25
				5	6				10	11	7			9	3					8		2			4		1					26
	2	3			6				10	11	7	5				4				8	12					9	1					27
				5	6		12		10	11	7			9	3*	4			14	8†		2					1					28
				5	6				10	11	7*			9†	3	4			12	8		2						1	14			29
				5	6				10	11	7			9†	3	4			12	8		2						1	4			30
				5					10	11	7				3		8*		12			2				6	9	1				31
				5					10	11	7				3		8		12			2*				6	9	1				32
				5					10	11	7				3		8					2				6	9	1				33
				5	6				10	11	7				3*	4	8†		12		14	2					9	1				34
				5*	6				10	11	7				3	4	8		12		14	2†					9	1				35
				5	6				10	11	7				3	4	8		12			2					9*	1				36
				5	6				10	11	7				3	4	8		12			2					9*	1				37
				5	6				10	11	7				3*	4	8		12		14	2					9†	1				38
					6				10	11*	7	5			3	4	8		12		14	2†					9	1				39
					6				10	11†	7	5			3	4	8		12			2*					9	1	14			40
				5	6				10	11	7				3	4	8					2					9	1				41
				5	6				10	11†	7				3	4	8		12			2*					9	1	14			42
				5*	6				10	11	7				3	4	8		12								9	1	2			43
				5	6				10	11	7				3	4	8		12								9	1	2*			44
					6				10	11	7	5				4	8*		12						14		9	1	2	3†		45
					6				10	8*	7	5				4			12			2					9		11	3†	14	46
12	18	21	3	37	37	17	30	8	27	37	29	25	14	15	9	20	7	10	13	22	1	19	23	2	3	11	16	15	4	1		
	1						2		5	4	7				5	5	3			1	1	1	1	1		14	3		2		1	
	2			3	3		11	2	9	8			7			1	1	2	2	2			4	1		1	7					

67

1970-71 SEASON

FIRST DIVISION

Arsenal	42	29	7	6	71	29	65
Leeds United	42	27	10	5	72	30	64
Tottenham Hotspur	42	19	14	9	54	33	52
Wolves	42	22	8	12	64	54	52
Liverpool	42	17	17	8	42	24	51
Chelsea	42	18	15	9	52	42	51
Southampton	42	17	12	13	56	44	46
Manchester United	42	16	11	15	65	66	43
Derby County	**42**	**16**	**10**	**16**	**56**	**54**	**42**
Coventry City	42	16	10	16	37	38	42
Manchester City	42	12	17	13	47	42	41
Newcastle United	42	14	13	15	44	46	41
Stoke City	42	12	13	17	44	48	37
Everton	42	12	13	17	54	60	37
Huddersfield Town	42	11	14	17	40	49	36
Nottingham Forest	42	14	8	20	42	61	36
West Brom. Albion	42	10	15	17	58	75	35
Crystal Palace	42	12	11	19	39	57	35
Ipswich Town	42	12	10	20	42	48	34
West Ham United	42	10	14	18	47	60	34
Burnley	42	7	13	22	29	63	27
Blackpool	42	4	15	23	34	66	23

1971-72 SEASON

FIRST DIVISION

Derby County	**42**	**24**	**10**	**8**	**69**	**33**	**58**
Leeds United	42	24	9	9	73	31	57
Liverpool	42	24	9	9	64	30	57
Manchester City	42	23	11	8	77	45	57
Arsenal	42	22	8	12	58	40	52
Tottenham Hotspur	42	19	13	10	63	42	51
Chelsea	42	18	12	12	58	49	48
Manchester United	42	19	10	13	69	61	48
Wolves	42	18	11	13	65	57	47
Sheffield United	42	17	12	13	61	60	46
Newcastle United	42	15	11	16	49	52	41
Leicester City	42	13	13	16	41	46	39
Ipswich Town	42	11	16	15	39	53	38
West Ham United	42	12	12	18	47	51	36
Everton	42	9	18	15	37	48	36
West Brom. Albion	42	12	11	19	42	54	35
Stoke City	42	10	15	17	39	56	35
Coventry City	42	9	15	18	44	67	33
Southampton	42	12	7	23	52	80	31
Crystal Palace	42	8	13	21	39	65	29
Nottingham Forest	42	8	9	25	47	81	25
Huddersfield Town	42	6	13	23	27	59	25

1972-73 SEASON

FIRST DIVISION

Liverpool	42	25	10	6	72	42	60
Arsenal	42	23	11	8	57	43	57
Leeds United	42	21	11	10	71	45	53
Ipswich Town	42	17	14	11	55	45	48
Wolves	42	18	11	13	66	54	47
West Ham United	42	17	12	13	67	53	46
Derby County	**42**	**19**	**8**	**15**	**56**	**54**	**46**
Tottenham Hotspur	42	16	13	13	58	48	45
Newcastle United	42	16	13	13	60	51	45
Birmingham City	42	15	12	15	53	54	42
Manchester City	42	15	11	16	57	60	41
Chelsea	42	13	14	15	49	51	40
Southampton	42	11	18	13	47	52	40
Sheffield United	42	15	10	17	51	59	40
Stoke City	42	14	10	18	61	56	38
Leicester City	42	10	17	15	40	46	37
Everton	42	13	11	18	41	49	37
Manchester United	42	12	13	17	44	60	37
Coventry City	42	13	9	20	40	55	35
Norwich City	42	11	10	21	36	63	32
Crystal Palace	42	9	12	21	41	58	30
West Brom. Albion	42	9	10	23	38	62	28

1973-74 SEASON

FIRST DIVISION

Leeds United	42	24	14	4	66	31	62
Liverpool	42	22	13	7	52	31	57
Derby County	**42**	**17**	**14**	**11**	**52**	**42**	**48**
Ipswich Town	42	18	11	13	67	58	47
Stoke City	42	15	16	11	54	42	46
Burnley	42	16	14	12	56	53	46
Everton	42	16	12	14	50	48	44
Q.P.R.	42	13	17	12	56	52	43
Leicester City	42	13	16	13	51	41	42
Arsenal	42	14	14	14	49	51	42
Tottenham Hotspur	42	14	14	14	45	50	42
Wolves	42	13	15	14	49	49	41
Sheffield United	42	14	12	16	44	49	40
Manchester City	42	14	12	16	39	46	40
Newcastle United	42	13	12	17	49	48	38
Coventry City	42	14	10	18	43	54	38
Chelsea	42	12	13	17	56	60	37
West Ham United	42	11	15	16	55	60	37
Birmingham City	42	12	13	17	52	64	37
Southampton *	42	11	14	17	47	68	36
Manchester United *	42	10	12	20	38	48	32
Norwich City *	42	7	15	20	37	62	29

* Three clubs relegated

1974-75 SEASON

FIRST DIVISION

Derby County	**42**	**21**	**11**	**10**	**67**	**49**	**53**
Liverpool	42	20	11	11	60	39	51
Ipswich Town	42	23	5	14	66	44	51
Everton	42	16	18	8	56	42	50
Stoke City	42	17	15	10	64	48	49
Sheffield United	42	18	13	11	58	51	49
Middlesbrough	42	18	12	12	54	40	48
Manchester City	42	18	10	14	54	54	46
Leeds United	42	16	13	13	57	49	45
Burnley	42	17	11	14	68	67	45
Q.P.R.	42	16	10	16	54	54	42
Wolves	42	14	11	17	57	54	39
West Ham United	42	13	13	16	58	59	39
Coventry City	42	12	15	15	51	62	39
Newcastle United	42	15	9	18	59	72	39
Arsenal	42	13	11	18	47	49	37
Birmingham City	42	14	9	19	53	61	37
Leicester City	42	12	12	18	46	60	36
Tottenham Hotspur	42	13	8	21	52	63	34
Luton Town	42	11	11	20	47	65	33
Chelsea	42	9	15	18	42	72	33
Carlisle United	42	12	5	25	43	59	29

1975-76 SEASON

FIRST DIVISION

Liverpool	42	23	14	5	66	31	60
Q.P.R.	42	24	11	7	67	33	59
Manchester United	42	23	10	10	68	42	56
Derby County	**42**	**21**	**11**	**10**	**75**	**58**	**53**
Leeds United	42	21	9	12	65	46	51
Ipswich Town	42	16	14	12	54	48	46
Leicester City	42	13	19	10	48	51	45
Manchester City	42	16	12	15	64	46	43
Tottenham Hotspur	42	14	15	13	63	63	43
Norwich City	42	16	10	16	58	58	42
Everton	42	15	12	15	60	66	42
Stoke City	42	15	11	16	48	50	41
Middlesbrough	42	15	10	17	46	45	40
Coventry City	42	13	14	15	47	57	40
Newcastle United	42	15	9	18	71	62	39
Aston Villa	42	11	17	14	51	59	39
Arsenal	42	13	10	19	47	53	36
West Ham United	42	13	10	19	48	71	36
Birmingham City	42	13	7	22	57	75	33
Wolves	42	10	10	22	51	68	30
Burnley	42	9	10	23	43	66	28
Sheffield United	42	6	10	26	33	82	22

1976-77 SEASON

FIRST DIVISION

Liverpool	42	23	11	8	62	33	57
Manchester City	42	21	14	7	60	34	56
Ipswich Town	42	22	8	12	66	39	52
Aston Villa	42	22	7	13	76	50	51
Newcastle United	42	18	13	11	64	49	49
Manchester United	42	18	11	13	71	62	47
West Brom. Albion	42	16	13	13	62	56	45
Arsenal	42	16	11	15	64	59	43
Everton	42	14	14	14	62	64	42
Leeds United	42	15	12	15	48	51	42
Leicester City	42	12	18	12	47	60	42
Middlesbrough	42	14	13	15	40	45	41
Birmingham City	42	13	12	17	63	61	38
Q.P.R.	42	13	12	17	47	52	38
Derby County	**42**	**9**	**19**	**14**	**50**	**55**	**37**
Norwich City	42	14	9	19	47	64	37
West Ham United	42	11	14	17	46	65	36
Bristol City	42	11	13	18	38	48	35
Coventry City	42	10	15	17	48	59	35
Sunderland	42	11	12	19	46	54	34
Stoke City	42	10	14	18	28	51	34
Tottenham Hotspur	42	12	9	21	48	72	33

1977-78 SEASON

FIRST DIVISION

Nottingham Forest	42	25	14	3	69	24	64
Liverpool	42	24	9	9	65	34	57
Everton	42	22	11	9	76	45	55
Manchester City	42	20	12	10	74	51	52
Arsenal	42	21	10	11	60	37	52
West Brom. Albion	42	18	14	10	62	53	50
Coventry City	42	18	12	12	75	62	48
Aston Villa	42	18	10	14	57	42	46
Leeds United	42	18	10	14	63	53	46
Manchester United	42	16	10	16	67	63	42
Birmingham City	42	16	9	17	55	60	41
Derby County	**42**	**14**	**13**	**15**	**54**	**59**	**41**
Norwich City	42	11	18	13	52	66	40
Middlesbrough	42	12	15	15	42	54	39
Wolves	42	12	12	18	51	64	36
Chelsea	42	11	14	17	46	69	36
Bristol City	42	11	13	18	49	53	35
Ipswich Town	42	11	13	18	47	61	35
Q.P.R.	42	9	15	18	47	64	33
West Ham United	42	12	8	22	52	69	32
Newcastle United	42	6	10	26	42	78	22
Leicester City	42	5	12	25	26	70	22

1978-79 SEASON

FIRST DIVISION

Liverpool	42	30	8	4	85	16	68
Nottingham Forest	42	21	18	3	61	26	60
West Brom. Albion	42	24	11	7	72	35	59
Everton	42	17	17	8	52	40	51
Leeds United	42	18	14	10	70	52	50
Ipswich Town	42	20	9	13	63	49	49
Arsenal	42	17	14	11	61	48	48
Aston Villa	42	15	16	11	59	49	46
Manchester United	42	15	15	12	60	63	45
Coventry City	42	14	16	12	58	68	44
Tottenham Hotspur	42	13	15	14	48	61	41
Middlesbrough	42	15	10	17	57	50	40
Bristol City	42	15	10	17	47	51	40
Southampton	42	12	16	14	47	53	40
Manchester City	42	13	13	16	58	56	39
Norwich City	42	7	23	12	51	57	37
Bolton Wanderers	42	12	11	19	54	75	35
Wolves	42	13	8	21	44	68	34
Derby County	**42**	**10**	**11**	**21**	**44**	**71**	**31**
Q.P.R.	42	6	13	23	45	73	25
Birmingham City	42	6	10	26	37	64	22
Chelsea	42	5	10	27	44	92	20

1979-80 SEASON

FIRST DIVISION

Liverpool	42	25	10	7	81	30	60
Manchester United	42	24	10	8	65	35	58
Ipswich Town	42	22	9	11	68	39	53
Arsenal	42	18	16	8	52	36	52
Nottingham Forest	42	20	8	14	63	43	48
Wolves	42	19	9	14	58	47	47
Aston Villa	42	16	14	12	51	50	46
Southampton	42	18	9	15	65	53	45
Middlesbrough	42	16	12	14	50	44	44
West Brom. Albion	42	11	19	12	54	50	41
Leeds United	42	13	14	15	46	50	40
Norwich City	42	13	14	15	58	66	40
Crystal Palace	42	12	16	14	41	50	40
Tottenham Hotspur	42	15	10	17	52	62	40
Coventry City	42	16	7	19	56	66	39
Brighton & Hove Alb.	42	11	15	16	47	57	37
Manchester City	42	12	13	17	43	66	37
Stoke City	42	13	10	19	44	58	36
Everton	42	9	17	16	43	51	35
Bristol City	42	9	13	20	37	66	31
Derby County	**42**	**11**	**8**	**23**	**47**	**67**	**30**
Bolton Wanderers	42	5	15	22	38	73	25

1980-81 SEASON

SECOND DIVISION

West Ham United	42	28	10	4	79	29	66
Notts County	42	18	17	7	49	38	53
Swansea City	42	18	14	10	64	44	50
Blackburn Rovers	42	16	18	8	42	29	50
Luton Town	42	18	12	12	61	46	48
Derby County	**42**	**15**	**15**	**12**	**57**	**52**	**45**
Grimsby Town	42	15	15	12	44	42	45
QPR	42	15	13	14	56	46	43
Watford	42	16	11	15	50	45	43
Sheffield Wednesday	42	17	8	17	53	51	42
Newcastle United	42	14	14	14	30	45	42
Chelsea	42	14	12	16	46	41	40
Cambridge United	42	17	6	17	53	65	40
Shrewsbury Town	42	11	17	14	46	47	39
Oldham Athletic	42	12	15	15	39	48	39
Wrexham	42	12	14	16	43	45	38
Orient	42	13	12	17	52	56	38
Bolton Wanderers	42	14	10	18	61	66	38
Cardiff City	42	12	12	18	44	60	36
Preston North End	42	11	14	17	41	62	36
Bristol City	42	7	16	19	29	51	30
Bristol Rovers	42	5	13	24	34	65	23

1981-82 SEASON

SECOND DIVISION

Luton Town	42	25	13	4	86	46	88
Watford	42	23	11	8	76	42	80
Norwich City	42	22	5	15	64	50	71
Sheffield Wednesday	42	20	10	12	55	51	70
QPR	42	21	6	15	65	43	69
Barnsley	42	19	10	13	59	41	67
Rotherham United	42	20	7	15	66	54	67
Leicester City	42	18	12	12	56	48	66
Newcastle United	42	18	8	16	52	50	62
Blackburn Rovers	42	16	11	15	47	43	59
Oldham Athletic	42	15	14	13	50	51	59
Chelsea	42	15	12	15	60	60	57
Charlton Athletic	42	13	12	17	50	65	51
Cambridge United	42	13	9	20	48	53	48
Crystal Palace	42	13	9	20	34	45	48
Derby County	**42**	**12**	**12**	**18**	**53**	**68**	**48**
Grimsby Town	42	11	13	18	53	65	46
Shrewsbury Town	42	11	3	18	37	57	46
Bolton Wanderers	42	13	7	22	39	61	46
Cardiff City	42	12	8	22	45	61	44
Wrexham	42	11	11	20	40	56	44
Orient	42	10	9	23	39	61	39

1982-83 SEASON

SECOND DIVISION

Q.P.R.	42	26	7	9	77	36	85
Wolves	42	20	15	7	68	44	75
Leicester City	42	20	10	12	72	44	70
Fulham *	42	20	9	13	64	47	69
Newcastle United	42	18	13	11	75	53	67
Sheffield Wednesday	42	16	15	11	60	47	63
Oldham Athletic	42	14	19	9	64	47	61
Leeds United	42	13	21	8	51	46	60
Shrewsbury Town	42	15	14	13	48	48	59
Barnsley	42	14	15	13	57	55	57
Blackburn Rovers	42	15	12	15	58	58	57
Cambridge United	42	13	12	17	42	60	51
Derby County *	**42**	**10**	**19**	**13**	**49**	**58**	**49**
Carlisle United	42	12	12	18	68	70	48
Crystal Palace	42	12	12	18	43	52	48
Middlesbrough	42	11	15	16	46	67	48
Charlton Athletic	42	13	9	20	63	86	48
Chelsea	42	11	14	17	51	61	47
Grimsby Town	42	12	11	19	45	70	47
Rotherham United	42	10	15	17	45	68	45
Burnley	42	12	8	22	56	66	44
Bolton Wanderers	42	11	11	20	42	61	44

* Game between Derby and Fulham abandoned after 88 minutes but result allowed to stand at 1-0.

1983-84 SEASON

SECOND DIVISION

Chelsea	42	25	13	4	90	40	88
Sheffield Wednesday	42	26	10	6	72	34	88
Newcastle United	42	24	8	10	85	53	80
Manchester City	42	20	10	12	66	48	70
Grimsby Town	42	19	13	10	60	47	70
Blackburn Rovers	42	17	16	9	57	46	67
Carlisle United	42	16	16	10	48	41	64
Shrewsbury Town	42	17	10	15	49	53	61
Brighton & Hove Alb.	42	17	9	16	69	60	60
Leeds United	42	16	12	14	55	56	60
Fulham	42	15	12	15	60	53	57
Huddersfield Town	42	14	15	13	56	49	57
Charlton Athletic	42	16	9	17	53	64	57
Barnsley	42	15	7	20	57	53	52
Cardiff City	42	15	6	21	53	66	51
Portsmouth	42	14	7	21	73	64	49
Middlesbrough	42	12	13	17	41	47	49
Crystal Palace	42	12	11	19	42	52	47
Oldham Athletic	42	13	8	21	47	73	47
Derby County	**42**	**11**	**9**	**22**	**36**	**72**	**42**
Swansea City	42	7	8	27	36	85	29
Cambridge United	42	4	12	26	28	77	24

1984-85 SEASON

THIRD DIVISION

Bradford City	46	28	10	8	77	45	94
Millwall	46	26	12	8	83	42	90
Hull City	46	25	12	9	88	49	87
Gillingham	46	25	8	13	80	62	83
Bristol City	46	24	9	13	74	47	81
Bristol Rovers	46	21	12	13	66	48	75
Derby County	**46**	**19**	**13**	**14**	**65**	**54**	**70**
York City	46	20	9	17	70	57	69
Reading	46	19	12	15	68	62	69
Bournemouth	46	19	11	16	57	46	68
Walsall	46	18	13	15	58	52	67
Rotherham United	46	18	11	17	55	55	65
Brentford	46	16	14	16	62	64	62
Doncaster Rovers	46	17	8	21	72	74	59
Plymouth Argyle	46	15	14	17	62	65	59
Wigan Athletic	46	15	14	17	60	64	59
Bolton Wanderers	46	16	6	24	69	75	54
Newport County	46	13	13	20	55	67	52
Lincoln City	46	11	18	17	50	51	51
Swansea City	46	12	11	23	53	80	47
Burnley	46	11	13	22	60	73	46
Orient	46	11	13	22	51	76	46
Preston North End	46	13	7	26	51	100	46
Cambridge United	46	4	9	33	37	95	21

1985-86 SEASON

THIRD DIVISION

Reading	46	29	7	10	67	50	94
Plymouth Argyle	46	26	9	11	88	53	87
Derby County	**46**	**23**	**15**	**8**	**80**	**41**	**84**
Wigan Athletic	46	23	14	9	82	48	83
Gillingham	46	22	13	11	81	54	79
Walsall	46	22	9	15	90	64	75
York City	46	20	11	15	77	58	71
Notts County	46	19	14	13	71	60	71
Bristol City	46	18	14	14	69	60	68
Brentford	46	18	12	16	58	61	66
Doncaster Rovers	46	16	16	14	45	52	64
Blackpool	46	17	12	17	66	55	63
Darlington	46	15	13	18	61	78	58
Rotherham United	46	15	12	19	61	59	57
Bournemouth	46	15	9	22	65	72	54
Bristol Rovers	46	14	12	20	51	75	54
Chesterfield	46	13	14	19	61	64	53
Bolton Wanderers	46	15	8	23	54	68	53
Newport County	46	11	18	17	52	65	51
Bury	46	12	13	21	63	65	49
Lincoln City	46	10	16	20	55	77	46
Cardiff City	46	12	9	25	53	83	45
Wolves	46	11	10	25	57	98	43
Swansea	46	11	10	25	43	87	43

1986-87 SEASON

SECOND DIVISION

Derby County	**42**	**25**	**9**	**8**	**64**	**38**	**84**
Portsmouth	42	23	9	10	53	28	78
Oldham Athletic	42	22	9	11	65	44	75
Leeds United	42	19	11	12	58	44	68
Ipswich Town	42	17	13	12	59	43	64
Crystal Palace	42	19	5	18	51	53	62
Plymouth Argyle	42	16	13	13	62	57	61
Stoke City	42	16	10	16	63	53	58
Sheffield United	42	15	13	14	50	49	58
Bradford City	42	15	10	17	62	62	55
Barnsley	42	14	13	15	49	52	55
Blackburn Rovers	42	15	10	17	45	55	55
Reading	42	14	11	17	52	59	53
Hull City	42	13	14	15	41	55	53
West Brom	42	13	12	17	51	49	51
Millwall	42	14	9	19	39	45	51
Huddersfield Town	42	13	12	17	54	61	51
Shrewsbury Town	42	15	6	21	41	63	51
Birmingham City	42	11	17	14	47	59	50
Sunderland	42	12	12	18	49	59	48
Grimsby Town	42	10	14	18	39	59	44
Brighton & Hove Alb.	42	9	12	21	37	54	39

1987-88 SEASON

FIRST DIVISION

Liverpool	40	26	12	2	87	24	90
Manchester United	40	23	12	5	71	38	81
Nottingham Forest	40	20	13	7	67	39	73
Everton	40	19	13	8	53	27	70
QPR	40	19	10	11	48	38	67
Arsenal	40	18	12	10	58	39	66
Wimbledon	40	14	15	11	58	47	57
Newcastle United	40	14	14	12	55	53	56
Luton Town	40	14	11	15	57	58	53
Coventry City	40	13	14	13	46	53	53
Sheffield Wednesday	40	15	8	17	52	66	53
Southampton	40	12	14	14	49	53	50
Tottenham Hotspur	40	12	11	17	38	48	47
Norwich City	40	12	9	19	40	52	45
Derby County	**40**	**10**	**13**	**17**	**35**	**45**	**43**
West Ham United	40	9	15	16	40	52	42
Charlton Athletic	40	9	15	16	38	52	42
Chelsea	40	9	15	16	50	68	42
Portsmouth	40	7	14	19	36	66	35
Watford	40	7	11	22	27	51	32
Oxford United	40	6	13	21	44	80	31

1988-89 SEASON

FIRST DIVISION

Arsenal	38	22	10	6	73	36	76
Liverpool	38	22	10	6	65	28	76
Nottingham Forest	38	17	13	8	64	43	64
Norwich City	38	17	11	10	48	45	62
Derby County	**38**	**17**	**7**	**14**	**40**	**38**	**58**
Tottenham Hotspur	38	15	12	11	60	46	57
Coventry City	38	14	13	11	47	42	55
Everton	38	14	12	12	50	45	54
QPR	38	14	11	13	43	37	53
Millwall	38	14	11	13	47	52	53
Manchester United	38	13	12	13	45	35	51
Wimbledon	38	14	9	15	50	46	51
Southampton	38	10	15	13	52	66	45
Charlton Athletic	38	10	12	16	44	58	42
Sheffield Wednesday	38	10	12	16	34	51	42
Luton Town	38	10	11	17	42	52	41
Aston Villa	38	9	13	16	45	56	40
Middlesbrough	38	9	12	17	44	61	39
West Ham United	38	10	8	20	37	62	38
Newcastle United	38	7	10	21	32	63	31

1989-90 SEASON

FIRST DIVISION

Liverpool	38	23	10	5	78	37	79
Aston Villa	38	21	7	10	57	38	70
Tottenham Hotspur	38	19	6	13	59	47	63
Arsenal	38	18	8	12	54	38	62
Chelsea	38	16	12	10	58	50	60
Everton	38	17	8	13	51	33	59
Southampton	38	15	10	13	71	63	55
Wimbledon	38	13	16	9	47	40	55
Nottingham Forest	38	15	9	14	55	47	54
Norwich City	38	13	14	11	44	42	53
QPR	38	13	11	14	45	44	50
Coventry City	38	14	7	17	39	59	49
Manchester United	38	13	9	16	46	47	48
Manchester City	38	12	12	14	43	52	48
Crystal Palace	38	13	9	16	42	66	48
Derby County	**38**	**13**	**7**	**18**	**43**	**40**	**46**
Luton Town	38	10	13	15	43	57	43
Sheffield Wednesday	38	11	10	17	35	51	43
Charlton Athletic	38	7	9	22	31	57	30
Millwall	38	5	11	22	39	65	26

1990-91 SEASON

FIRST DIVISION

Team	P	W	D	L	F	A	Pts
Arsenal	38	24	13	1	74	18	83
Liverpool	38	23	7	8	77	40	76
Crystal Palace	38	20	9	9	50	41	69
Leeds United	38	19	7	12	65	47	64
Manchester City	38	17	11	10	64	53	62
Manchester United	38	16	12	10	58	45	59
Wimbledon	38	14	14	10	53	46	56
Nottingham Forest	38	14	12	12	65	50	54
Everton	38	13	12	13	50	46	51
Tottenham	38	11	16	11	51	50	49
Chelsea	38	13	10	15	58	69	49
QPR	38	12	10	16	44	53	46
Sheffield United	38	13	7	18	36	55	46
Southampton	38	12	9	17	58	69	45
Norwich City	38	13	6	19	41	64	45
Coventry City	38	11	11	16	42	49	44
Aston Villa	38	9	14	15	46	58	41
Luton Town	38	10	7	21	42	61	37
Sunderland	38	8	10	20	38	60	34
Derby County	**38**	**5**	**9**	**24**	**37**	**75**	**24**

Arsenal 2 points deducted
Manchester United 1 point deducted

1991-92 SEASON

SECOND DIVISION

Team	P	W	D	L	F	A	Pts
Ipswich Town	46	24	12	10	70	50	84
Middlesbrough	46	23	11	12	58	41	80
Derby County	**46**	**23**	**9**	**14**	**69**	**51**	**78**
Leicester City	46	23	8	15	62	55	77
Cambridge United	46	19	17	10	65	47	74
Blackburn Rvrs	46	21	11	14	70	53	74
Charlton Athletic	46	20	11	15	54	48	71
Swindon Town	46	18	15	13	69	55	69
Portsmouth	46	19	12	15	65	51	69
Watford	46	18	11	17	51	48	65
Wolves	46	18	10	18	61	54	64
Southend United	46	17	11	18	63	63	62
Bristol Rovers	46	16	14	16	60	63	62
Tranmere Rovers	46	14	19	13	56	56	61
Millwall	46	17	10	19	64	71	61
Barnsley	46	16	11	19	46	57	59
Bristol City	46	13	15	18	55	71	54
Sunderland	46	14	11	21	61	65	53
Grimsby Town	46	14	11	21	47	62	53
Newcastle United	46	13	13	20	66	84	52
Oxford United	46	13	11	22	66	73	50
Plymouth Argyle	46	13	9	24	42	64	48
Brighton & Hove Alb.	46	12	11	23	56	77	47
Port Vale	46	10	15	21	42	59	45

1992-93 SEASON

FIRST DIVISION

Team	P	W	D	L	F	A	Pts
Newcastle United	46	29	9	8	92	38	96
West Ham United	46	26	10	10	81	41	88
Portsmouth	46	26	10	10	80	46	88
Tranmere Rovers	46	23	10	13	72	56	79
Swindon Town	46	21	13	12	74	59	76
Leicester City	46	22	10	14	71	64	76
Millwall	46	18	16	12	65	53	70
Derby County	**46**	**19**	**9**	**18**	**68**	**57**	**66**
Grimsby Town	46	19	7	20	58	57	64
Peterborough United	46	16	14	16	55	63	62
Wolves	46	16	13	17	57	56	61
Charlton Athletic	46	16	13	17	49	46	61
Barnsley	46	17	9	20	56	60	60
Oxford United	46	14	14	18	53	56	56
Bristol City	46	14	14	18	49	67	56
Watford	46	14	13	19	57	71	55
Notts County	46	12	16	18	55	70	52
Southend United	46	13	13	20	54	64	52
Birmingham City	46	13	12	21	50	72	51
Luton Town	46	10	21	15	48	62	51
Sunderland	46	13	11	22	50	64	50
Brentford	46	13	10	23	52	71	49
Cambridge United	46	11	16	19	48	69	49
Bristol Rovers	46	10	11	25	55	87	41

1993-94 SEASON

FIRST DIVISION

Team	P	W	D	L	F	A	Pts
Crystal Palace	46	27	9	10	73	46	90
Nottingham Forest	46	23	14	9	74	49	83
Millwall	46	19	17	10	58	49	74
Leicester City	46	19	16	11	72	59	73
Tranmere Rovers	46	21	9	16	69	53	72
Derby County	**46**	**20**	**11**	**15**	**73**	**68**	**71**
Notts County	46	20	7	19	65	69	68
Wolves	46	17	17	12	60	47	68
Middlesbrough	46	18	13	15	66	54	67
Stoke City	46	18	13	15	57	59	67
Charlton Athletic	46	19	8	19	61	58	65
Sunderland	46	19	8	19	54	57	65
Bristol City	46	16	16	14	47	50	64
Bolton Wanderers	46	15	14	17	63	64	59
Southend United	46	17	8	21	63	67	59
Grimsby Town	46	13	20	13	52	47	59
Portsmouth	46	15	13	18	52	58	58
Barnsley	46	16	7	23	55	67	55
Watford	46	15	9	22	66	80	54
Luton Town	46	14	11	21	56	60	53
West Brom. Albion	46	13	12	21	60	69	51
Birmingham City	46	13	12	21	52	69	51
Oxford United	46	13	10	23	54	75	49
Peterborough United	46	8	13	25	48	76	37

1993-94 SEASON

FIRST DIVISION

Team	P	W	D	L	F	A	Pts
Middlesbrough	46	23	13	10	67	40	82
Reading	46	23	10	13	58	44	79
Bolton Wanderers	46	21	14	11	67	45	76
Wolves	46	21	13	12	77	61	76
Tranmere Rovers	46	22	10	14	67	58	76
Barnsley	46	20	12	14	63	52	72
Watford	46	19	13	14	52	46	70
Sheffield United	46	17	17	12	74	55	68
Derby County	**46**	**18**	**12**	**16**	**66**	**51**	**66**
Grimsby Town	46	17	14	15	62	56	65
Stoke City	46	16	15	15	50	53	63
Millwall	46	16	14	16	60	60	62
Southend United	46	18	8	20	54	73	62
Oldham Athletic	46	16	13	17	60	60	61
Charlton Athletic	46	16	11	19	58	66	59
Luton Town	46	15	13	18	61	64	58
Port Vale	46	15	13	18	58	64	58
Portsmouth	46	15	13	18	53	63	58
West Brom. Albion	46	16	10	20	51	57	58
Sunderland	46	12	18	16	41	45	54
Swindon Town	46	12	12	22	54	73	48
Burnley	46	11	13	22	49	74	46
Bristol City	46	11	12	23	42	63	45
Notts County	46	9	13	24	45	66	40